Getting Down To Business In English
Students' Book 1

CHRISTOPHER PEARSON

Illustrations by
Peter Edwards

HEINEMANN EDUCATIONAL BOOKS
LONDON

Heinemann Educational Books Ltd
22 Bedford Square, London WC1B 3HH

LONDON   EDINBURGH   MELBOURNE   AUCKLAND
HONG KONG   SINGAPORE   KUALA LUMPUR   NEW DELHI
IBADAN   NAIROBI   JOHANNESBURG
EXETER (NH)   KINGSTON   PORT OF SPAIN

ISBN 0 435 28690 0

© Christopher Pearson 1974
First published 1974
Reprinted 1977, 1979, 1980

Printed in Great Britain by Spottiswoode Ballantyne Ltd.
Colchester and London

Introduction

Getting Down to Business in English is a two-book course for students who have a practical need for English in their work or social life. Many such students may have learned some English before but will have forgotten most of it. At the outset, therefore, the course is elementary. It assumes very little previous knowledge of the language on the one hand and a fairly high motivation to learn on the other. While maintaining the careful grading characteristic of modern language teaching, the course moves rapidly through the basic structural features of English.

Because the course is directed at the functional needs of the learner, it ensures that the student is able to use the English he is learning from early on.

Among the many situations covered in Book 1 are travel, offices, banks, restaurants, hotels, buying and selling goods, using the telephone and simple letter-writing.

Notes

Mask

A coloured mask is attached to the back copy of this book and full instructions on its use are given in the Teachers' Book.

Teachers' Book

A separate Teachers' Book is available to accompany Students' Book One. The way to approach the teaching of the material is outlined in the *General Introduction, Design of the Course* and *The General Teaching Plan*. This is followed by practical lesson-by-lesson notes under the general headings of *Purpose, Preliminary Work, Reading* or *Conversation, Exercises, Further Exercises* not presented in the Students' Book and *Homework*.

Recorded Material

All the *Readings* and *Conversations* which begin each lesson have been recorded and are available on tape. So too, are most of the *Exercises* in the Students' Book. Recorded exercises are indicated in both the Students' Book and the Teachers' Book with the symbol

1

This is a travel-agency.

2

Who's this?
What is she?

It's Mary Fletcher.
She's a secretary.

3

Who's this?
What is he?

It's Mr Davis.
He's the manager.

4

What's Mr Davis
saying?

He's saying: 'Come in,
Miss Fletcher.'

5

What's he saying
now?

He's saying: 'Close the
door, please.'

6

And now?

'Sit down, please.'

7

And now?

'Take your pencil and your pad.'

8

What's Miss Fletcher doing?

She's writing a letter in shorthand.

9

What's Mr Davis doing?

He's dictating the letter.

10

What's he saying now?

He's saying: 'Type the letter, Miss Fletcher.'

11

What's Miss Fletcher doing now?

She's typing the letter.

12

What's she saying now?

She's saying: 'Sign the letter please, Mr Davis.'

13

What's Mr Davis doing?

He's signing the letter.

14

Who's this?
What is he?

It's Peter.
He's a booking clerk.

15

And who's this?
What is he?

It's Mr Barratt.
He's a customer.

16

What's Peter saying?

He's saying: 'Good morning, sir.'

17

What's Mr Barratt saying?

He's saying: 'Book this journey, please.'

18

And what's Peter saying?

He's saying: 'Certainly, sir.'

19

What's Peter
doing now?

He's going out. He's
going to the airline
office.

20

And what's Mary
doing?

She's going out too.
She's going to the
post-office.

21

What are Peter and
Mary saying?

They're saying:
'Goodbye Peter.'
'Goodbye Mary.'

Exercise A	Is Mary a secretary?	Yes, she is.
	Is Mr Davis the manager?	Yes, he is.
	Is Peter the manager?	No, he isn't.
	Is Mary a booking clerk?	No, she isn't.
	In Picture 4 is Mr Davis saying: 'Sit down, Miss Fletcher'?	No, he isn't.
	Are Mary and Peter managers?	No, they aren't.
	In Picture 11, is Mary typing a letter?	Yes, she is.
	In Picture 12, is Mary typing a letter?	No, she isn't.
	In Picture 19 is Peter going out?	Yes, he is.
	In Pictures 19 and 20, are Peter and Mary going out?	Yes, they are.
	Is Peter going to the post-office?	No, he isn't.
	Is Mary going to the post-office?	Yes, she is.

4

Mary's in the office.

Peter's at the counter.

1

Mary: Peter, what are you doing?

Peter: I'm booking a journey for Mr Johnson

2

Mary: But what are you doing now?

Peter: I'm putting a letter in an envelope.

3

Mary: Are you putting a stamp on it?

Peter: Yes, I am. What are you doing, Mary?

4

Mary: I'm typing a letter for Mr Davis.

Peter: Mr Davis is coming.

Mr Davis is in the office now.

5

Mr Davis: What are you doing, Miss Fletcher?

Mary: I'm finishing this letter.

6

Mr Davis: What are you doing, Peter?

Peter: I'm putting a ticket in a passport.

7

Mr Davis: Are you and Mary working?

Mary and Peter: Yes, we are, we're working.

8

Mr Davis: You're talking, too.

Mary: Yes, we're talking, but we're working.

9

Mr Davis: Goodbye.

Peter and Mary: Goodbye.

Mr Davis is leaving the office.

10

Peter: Where's he going?

Mary: He's going home.

11

Peter: Isn't he signing the letter, today?

Mary: No, he's not.

12

Peter: Then we're going home, too.

Mary: All right. We're leaving now.

Exercise B

1. In Picture 1, what's Peter doing?
2. In Picture 2, is he putting a ticket in a passport?
3. In Picture 3, is he putting a stamp on the envelope?
4. In Picture 4, what's Mary doing?
5. Are Mary and Peter working?
6. Is Mr Davis working?
7. Is he signing the letters today?
8. In Picture 12, are Mary and Peter going home?
9. Are you working now?
10. Are you talking now?
11. Are you typing?
12. Are you leaving now?

Exercise C   Listen to your teacher.

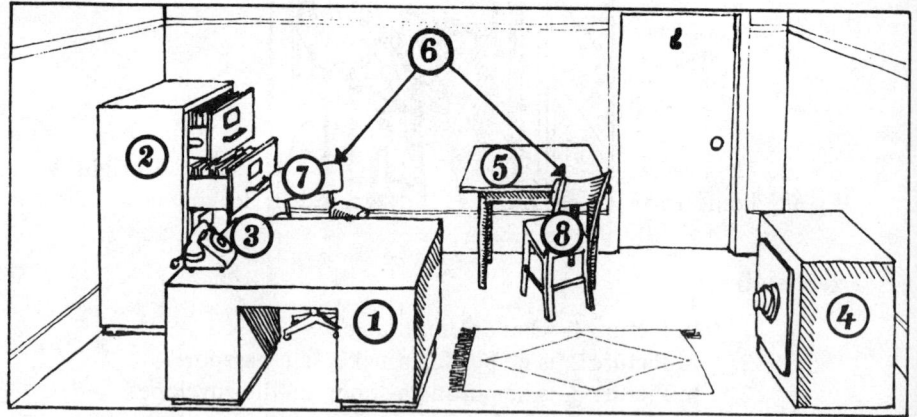

What is there on this page?	There's a picture.
What is there in the picture?	There's an office.
What is there in the office?	(1) There's a desk.
	(2) There's a filing cabinet.
	(3) There's a telephone.
	(4) There's a safe.
	(5) There's a small table.
	(6) There are two chairs.

Exercise D   Listen to your teacher.

What is there in the office?	(1) There's a desk in the middle.
	(2) There's a filing cabinet in the corner on the left.
	(3) There's a telephone on the desk.
	(4) There's a safe on the right.
	(5) There's a small table behind the door.
	(6) There are two chairs.
	(7) There's one chair behind the desk.
	(8) There's another in front of the table.

Exercise E   Listen to your teacher.

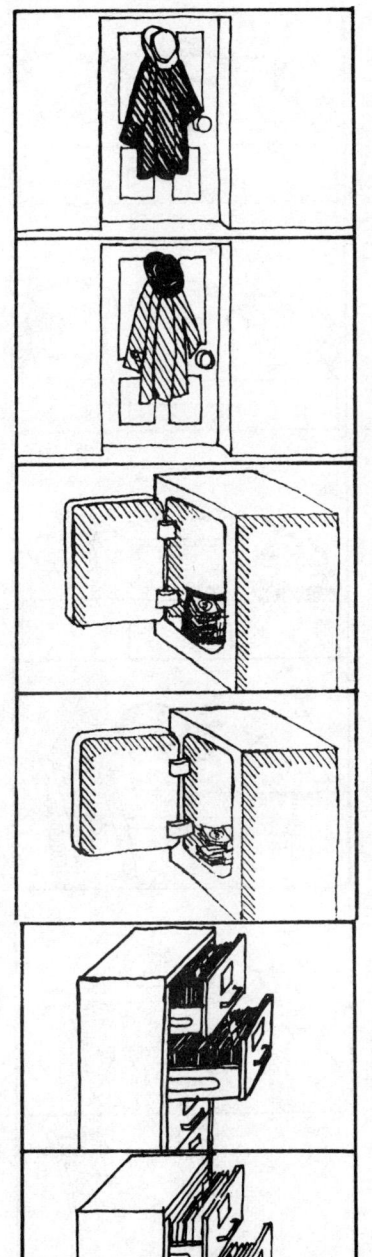

Is there anything on
the door?

Yes, there is.
Yes, there's something
on the door.
There's a coat on the
door.

Is there anything else
on the door?

Yes, there is.
Yes, there's something
else on the door.
There's a hat on the
door too.

Is there anything in
the safe?

Yes, there is.
Yes, there's something
in the safe.
There's some money in
the safe.

Is there anything else
in the safe?

No, there isn't.
No, there's nothing
else in the safe.

Is there anything in the
filing-cabinet?

Yes, there is.
Yes, there's something
in the filing-cabinet.
There are some files in
the filing-cabinet.

Is there anything else
in there?

No, there isn't.
No, there isn't anything
else in the
filing-cabinet.

Is there anything on the desk?

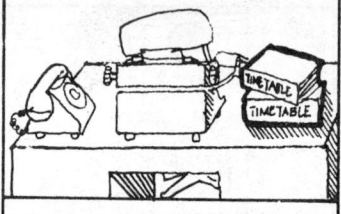

Yes, there is.
Yes, there's something on the desk.
There's a typewriter on the desk.

Is there anything else on the desk?

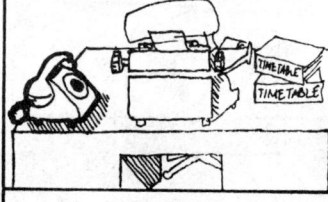

Yes, there is.
Yes, there's something else on the desk.
There are two timetables on the desk too.

Is there anything else on the desk?

Yes there is.
Yes, there's something else on the desk.
There's a telephone on the desk.

Is there anything on the small table?

Yes, there is.
There's an ashtray on the small table.

Is there anything else on the small table?

Yes, there is.
There's a packet of cigarettes on the small table.

Is there anything on the chairs?

No, there isn't.
There's nothing on the chairs.
There isn't anything on the chairs.

Is there anything under
the table?
Is there a book?

No, there isn't.
No, there isn't a book
under the table.
There's not a book
under the table.

Is there anything on
the ceiling?

Yes, there is.
Yes, there is something
on the ceiling.
There are two lights on
the ceiling.

Exercise F   Listen to your teacher.

Is there anybody in
this picture?

Yes, there is.
There's somebody in the
picture.
It's Miss Brown.

Is there anybody in
this picture?

No, there isn't.
There's nobody in the
picture.

Exercise G   Listen to your teacher.

It's one o'clock.
Jean Brown is leaving
the office.

She leaves the office at
one o'clock every day.

She's going to the shops.

She goes to the shops
every day.

She's going to the
butcher's.

She goes to the butcher's
every Friday.

She's buying some meat.

She buys meat every
Friday.
She buys it once a week.

She's not paying for
the meat now.

She pays for the meat
once a month.

Now Jean's standing
in front of the cafe.
Here's Caroline.

Jean and Caroline
meet every Friday.

They're having lunch together.

They have lunch together every **Friday**.

Caroline is ordering chips.
Jean is ordering salad.

She orders chips every time.
She orders salad every time.

The waiter is bringing the chips and the salad.

He brings chips for Caroline and salad for Jean every time.

Jean isn't eating any chips.

She doesn't eat chips.
She doesn't want to get fat.

Caroline is eating the chips. She's getting fat.

She doesn't mind.

Jean is drinking her coffee without sugar.

She drinks coffee without sugar. She doesn't drink coffee with sugar.

Exercise H Look at the following examples:

Does Jean leave the office at one o'clock every day?
Yes, she does.

Does Jean eat chips?
No, she doesn't.

Do Jean and Caroline meet every Friday?
Yes, they do.

Do they meet every Sunday?
No, they don't.

Now answer these questions, but don't look at the sentences on the right of the pictures.

1. Does Jean go to the shops every day?
2. Does she go to the butcher's every Friday?
3. Does she buy meat every Friday?
4. Does she pay for it every Friday?
5. Does she pay for it once a month?
6. Do Jean and Caroline meet every Friday?
7. Do they have lunch together every Friday?
8. Does Caroline order chips?
9. Does Jean eat chips?
10. Does Jean eat salad every time?
11. Does the waiter bring the chips and the salad?
12. Caroline's getting fat. Does she mind?
13. Do Jean and Caroline drink coffee?
14. Does Jean drink coffee with sugar?
15. Does she drink coffee without sugar?

Exercise I Answer these questions. Don't look at the sentences on the right of the pictures.

1. When does Jean leave the office every day?
2. Where does she go every day?
3. Where does she go every Friday?
4. What does she buy?
5. When does she pay for the meat?
6. Where do Jean and Caroline meet?
7. What do they do together every Friday?
8. What does Caroline eat?
9. What does the waiter bring for Jean?
10. How does Jean drink her coffee?

Exercise J Listen to your teacher.

Mr Williams is staying on business in Madrid. He's working at a bank.

What does he do at
seven o'clock?

He gets up.

What does he do next?

He goes to the
bathroom.

What does he do there?

He shaves and has
a bath.

What does he do next?

He dresses.

And then?

He has his breakfast.

When does he leave
the hotel?

He leaves the hotel at
eight o'clock.

When does he arrive at the bank?　　He arrives there at half past eight.

What time does the manager arrive?　　He arrives at half past nine.

Exercise K　Look at these sentences.

Mr Williams gets up at seven o'clock, but he's not getting up now.
Mr Williams shaves every day, but he's not shaving now.

Form similar sentences from these words.

1. Jean — go — to the butcher's every Friday　(Today)
2. Jean — have — lunch with Caroline every Friday　(Today)
3. The Waiter — bring — chips for Caroline every time　(Today)
4. Mr Williams — dress — every morning　(Today)
5. Jean — order — coffee every time　(Today)
6. Caroline — take — sugar in her coffee every morning　(Today)
7. Mr Williams — have — breakfast at half past seven　(Now)
8. Mr Williams — arrive — at the bank at half-past eight　(Now)
9. They — have — coffee together every Tuesday　(Now)
10. The manager — arrive — at half-past nine　(Now)

Exercise L　Listen to your teacher.

16

Today Jean goes to the tobacconist's.

She says:
'Have you got any French cigarettes?'

The shop-assistant says:
'No, we haven't, I'm sorry. We haven't got any French cigarettes.'

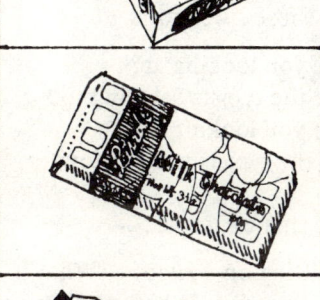

'What cigarettes have you got then?'

'We've only got English cigarettes.'

'Have you got any chocolate?'

'Yes, Madam, we have.'

(She looks into her handbag)
'Oh, dear. I haven't got any money. Goodbye.'

She hasn't got any money!
Some girls haven't got any sense.

Exercise M   Answer these questions.

1. Has the shop-assistant got any French cigarettes?
2. Has the shopkeeper got any chocolate?
3. Has Jean got any money?
4. What haven't some girls got?
5. Have you got any cigarettes?
6. Have you got any money?

Exercise N   Listen to your teacher.

1. Look at this picture.
2. The two typists are listening to dictaphones.
3. The dictaphones have got headphones. Look for them.
4. The typists are waiting for the manager.

Exercise O Answer these questions.

1. What are you looking at?
2. What are the typists listening to?
3. What are you looking for?
 4. Who are the typists waiting for?

Exercise P Look at this example:

Type A: John is sitting on *a chair*. (What?)
Type B: I beg your pardon. What is he sitting on?

Now turn these Type A expressions into Type B expressions.

1. Miss Brown is looking for *a pencil*. (What?)
2. I'm listening to *this dictaphone*. (What?)
3. He's dictating a letter to *the secretary*. (Who?)
4. I'm waiting for *the coffee*. (What?)
5. John is taking the letters to *the post-office*. (Where?)
6. I'm waiting for *the manager*. (Who?)
7. Mr Dean is standing on *the table*. (What?)
8. Caroline drinks coffee with *sugar*. (What?)
9. John is putting the ticket in *an envelope*. (What?)
10. I'm saying this to *my secretary*. (Who? . . . you . . .)
11. Jean pays for *the meat* once a month. (What?)
12. That student's looking at *another lesson*. (What?)

Exercise Q Listen to your teacher.

What nationality is
Peter?
Where does he come
from?
What is he?

He's British.
He comes from England.
He's an Englishman.

What nationality is
Jim?
Where does he come
from?
What is he?

He's American.
He comes from the
United States.
He's an American.

What nationality is
Colette?
Where does she come
from?
What is she?

She's French.
She comes from France.
She's a Frenchwoman.

What nationality is
Juan?
Where does he come
from?
What is he?

He's Spanish.
He comes from Spain.
He's a Spaniard.

What nationality is
Giuseppe?
Where does he come
from?
What is he?

He's Italian.
He comes from Italy.
He's an Italian.

What nationality is
Stavros?
Where does he come
from?
What is he?

He's Greek.
He comes from Greece.
He's a Greek.

What nationality is Mai Britt? Where does she come from? What is she?		She's Swedish. She comes from Sweden. She's a Swede.
What nationality is Celso? Where does he come from? What is he?		He's Brazilian. He comes from Brazil. He's a Brazilian.
What nationality is Consuelo? Where does she come from? What is she?		She's Argentine. She comes from Argentina. She's an Argentine.
What nationality is Manoel? Where does he come from? What is he?		He's Portuguese. He comes from Portugal. He's a Portuguese.

Conversation 1

Jim is introducing Juan to Colette:

Jim: Colette, this is Juan. Juan this is Colette.
Juan: How do you do?
Colette: How do you do.

Conversation 2

Celso knows Stavros.

Celso

'Good afternoon,
Stavros.'

'Very well, thank you.
How are you?'

'How are your mother
and father, Stavros?'

'Well, goodbye, Stavros.
Nice to see you.'

Stavros

'Good afternoon, Celso.
How are you?'

'Quite well, thanks.'

They're well, too,
thank you.'

'Same to you, Celso.
Goodbye.'

A man

Men

A woman

Women

This is a person.

These are people.

Mr and Mrs Davis
have got a son.
His name's Donald.

He's a child. He's ten
years old.

They've got a daughter
too.
Her name's Jill.

She's a child. She's
seven years old.

They've got a baby too.
His name's Alan.
He's six months old.

The Davises have got
three children.

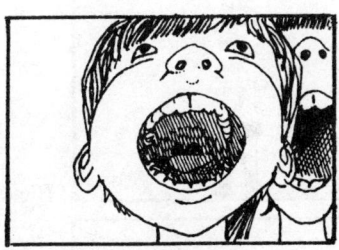

Donald and Jill have
got good teeth.

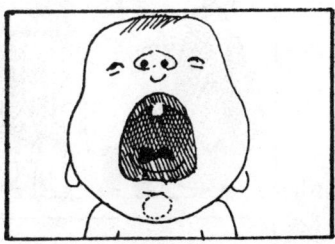

Alan's got one tooth.

Exercise R   Listen to your teacher and look at these pictures.

First

Second

Third

Fourth

Fifth

Sixth

Seventh

Eighth

Ninth

Tenth

Eleventh

Twelfth

Now look at these pictures.

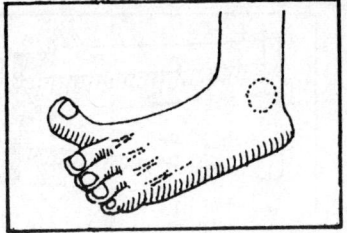

This is a foot.

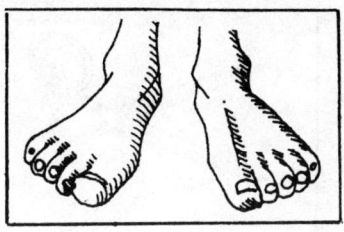

This is a pair of feet.

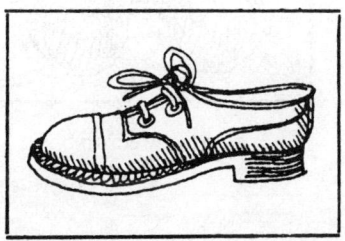

This is a shoe.

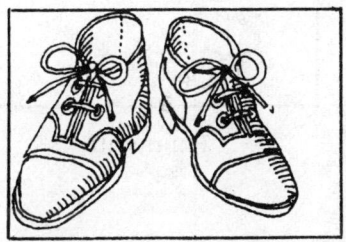

This is a pair of shoes.

This is a pair of spectacles.

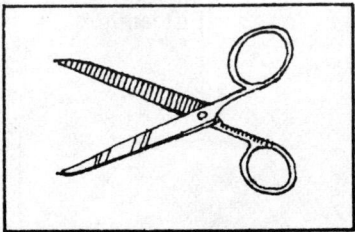

This is a pair of scissors.

Exercise S. Listen to your teacher and look at the pictures.

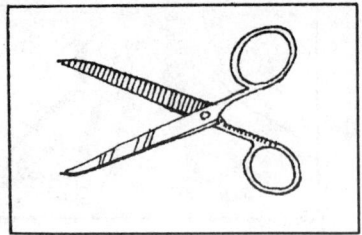

Thirteenth

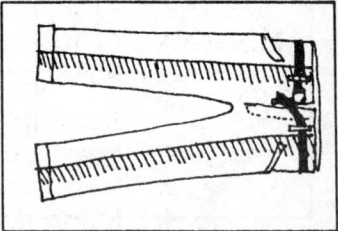

Sixteenth

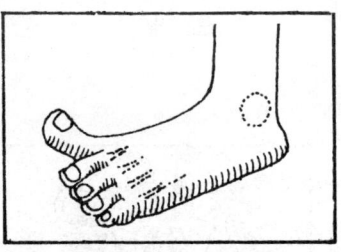

Fourteenth

Seventeenth

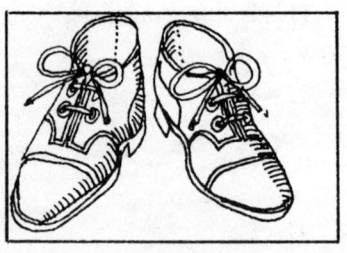

Fifteenth

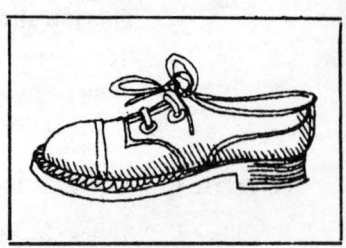

Eighteenth

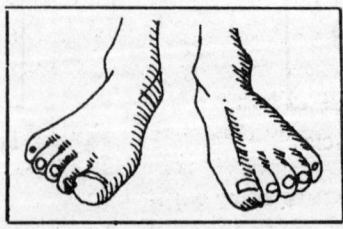

Nineteenth

Test for Lessons One to Ten

Exercise A   In each sentence, give the correct form of the verb in brackets.

1. Jean is British. She ... from England.   (come)
2. Jean ... Caroline every Friday.   (meet)
3. John ... to the post-office now.   (go)
4. It's eight o'clock. Mr Williams ...   (shave)
5. Mr Dean ... coffee with sugar every time.   (drink)
6. Celso ... Stavros.   (know)
7. Juan ... Colette to Stavros now.   (introduce)
8. Mrs Brown ... in the office now.   (sit)

Exercise B   Look at these sentences.

Type P.   I'm looking at *a file*   (What)
Type Q.   I beg your pardon. What are you looking at?

Now turn these Type P sentences into Type Q sentences.

1. He's going to *the post-office*.   (Where)
2. They've got *good teeth*.   (What)
3. Caroline is drinking *coffee*.   (What)
4. They sell *French cigarettes*.   (What)
5. I'm putting the trays in the *filing cabinet*.   (What)
6. We're waiting for *Jean*.   (Who)
7. I'm putting your coat *on the door*.   (Where)
8. He listens to *the dictaphone*.   (What)
9. Jean's paying for *the meat*.   (What)

Exercise C   Look at these sentences.

Type R.   Does she buy meat at the butcher's?   (No)
Type S.   No, she doesn't.

Type R.   Are you the manager?   (Yes)
Type S.   Yes, I am.

Now reply to these Type R sentences in the same way.

1. Do you take the letters to the post-office every day?   (Yes)
2. Does he come from Argentina?   (No)
3. Are you Brazilian?   (No)
4. Are they eating chocolate?   (Yes)
5. Has he got a pair of trousers?   (Yes)
6. Do you shave every day?   (Yes)
7. Are you looking for a pair of spectacles?   (No)
8. Do they sell French cigarettes at the tobacconist's?   (Yes)

Exercise D   Look at these sentences.

Type T.   Have you got any money?
Type U.   Yes, I have. I've got some money.

Now turn these Type T sentences into Type U sentences.

1. Have they got any French cigarettes at the tobacconist's?
2. Is there any sugar in my coffee?
3. Do you want any pencils?
4. Are there any files in the safe?

Exercise E   Look at these sentences.

Type V.   I've got some money.
Type W.   Oh, no you haven't. You haven't got any money.

Now turn these Type V sentences into Type W sentences.

1. There are some envelopes on the desk.
2. I've got some chocolate in my handbag.
3. There's somebody in the bathroom.
4. There are some people in the bank.

Vocabulary introduced in Lessons 1 to 10

across	ask	book (v)	ceiling
after	at	booking clerk	certainly
airline-office	baby	Brazil	chair
American	bank	Brazilian	child
another	bath	breakfast	chips
answer (v)	bathroom	bring	chocolate
anything	before	British	cigarette
Argentina	behind	business	clerk
Argentine	bicycle	butcher's	close (v)
arrive	blackboard	buy	coat
ashtray	book (n)	cafe	come

corner
coffee
count (v)
counter
cover
customer
daughter
desk
dictaphone
dictate
door
dress (v)
drink (v)
eat
England
English
Englishman
Englishwoman
envelope
every day
every time
fat
father
file
filing-cabinet
finish (v)
foot
for
France
French
Frenchman
Frenchwoman
Friday
get
get up
girl
give
go
good afternoon
goodbye
good morning
Greece
Greek
half past
handbag
hat

headphones
home
How are you?
How do you do?
I beg your pardon
I'm sorry
in
in front of
into
in the middle
introduce
Italian
Italy
journey
know
leave (v)
lesson
letter
light
listen
look
lunch
Madam
man
manager
meat
meet
mind (v)
Monday
money
month
mother
name
nationality
near
next
Nice to see you
nobody
nothing
now
o'clock
office
office-boy
on
on the left
on the right

once a week
only
open (v)
order (v)
packet
pad
page
pair
passport
pay (v)
pen
pencil
people
person
picture
place
Portugal
Portuguese
post-office
put
Quite well, thanks
safe
salad
Same to you
Saturday
say
scissors
secretary
sell
sense
sentence
shave
shoe
shop
shop-assistant
shorthand
sign
sit
small
son
Spaniard
Spain
spectacles
stand
stamp
street

student
sugar
Sunday
Swede
Swedish
table
take
talk (v)
teacher
telephone
then
there
Thursday
ticket
timetable
tobacconist's
today
together
too
tooth
travel agency
tray
trousers
Tuesday
type
typist
typewriter
under
United States
wait for
waiter
wall
want
Wednesday
well
what time
when
with
without
woman
work (v)
write
year.

Mr Gray's a grocer. He's ordering stock from a wholesaler.

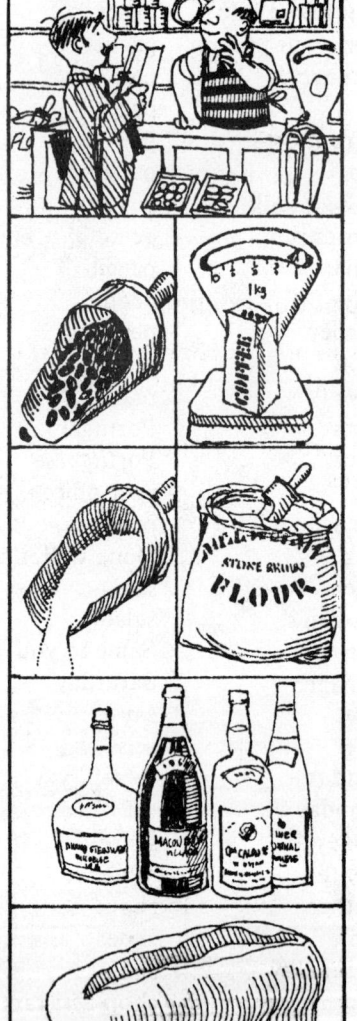

What's he ordering?

He's ordering some coffee.

We order coffee in kilos.

He's ordering some flour.

We order flour in bags.

He's ordering some wine.

We order wine in bottles.

He's ordering some bread.

We order bread in loaves.

He's ordering some razor-blades.

We order razor-blades in packets.

Exercise T   Look at these sentences.

Type M.   We buy coffee in kilos. What's Mr Gray buying   (1,000)
Type N.   He's buying a thousand kilos of coffee.

Now change the following Type M sentences into Type N answers:

1.   We buy flour in bags. What's Mr Gray buying?   (200)
2.   We buy wine in bottles. What's Mr Gray buying?   (24)
3.   We buy bread in loaves. What's Mr Gray buying?   (100)
4.   We buy razor-blades in packets. What's Mr Gray buying?   (2,000)

Exercise U   Now look at this example.

Question.   We buy ink in bottles. How do you buy ink?
Answer.   When I buy ink, I buy a bottle of ink.

Now form similar questions and answers from these words and pictures.

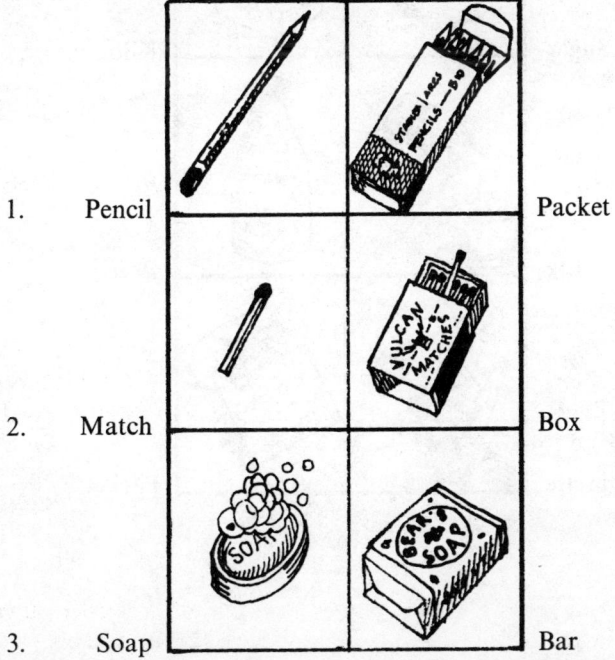

1.   Pencil   Packet

2.   Match   Box

3.   Soap   Bar

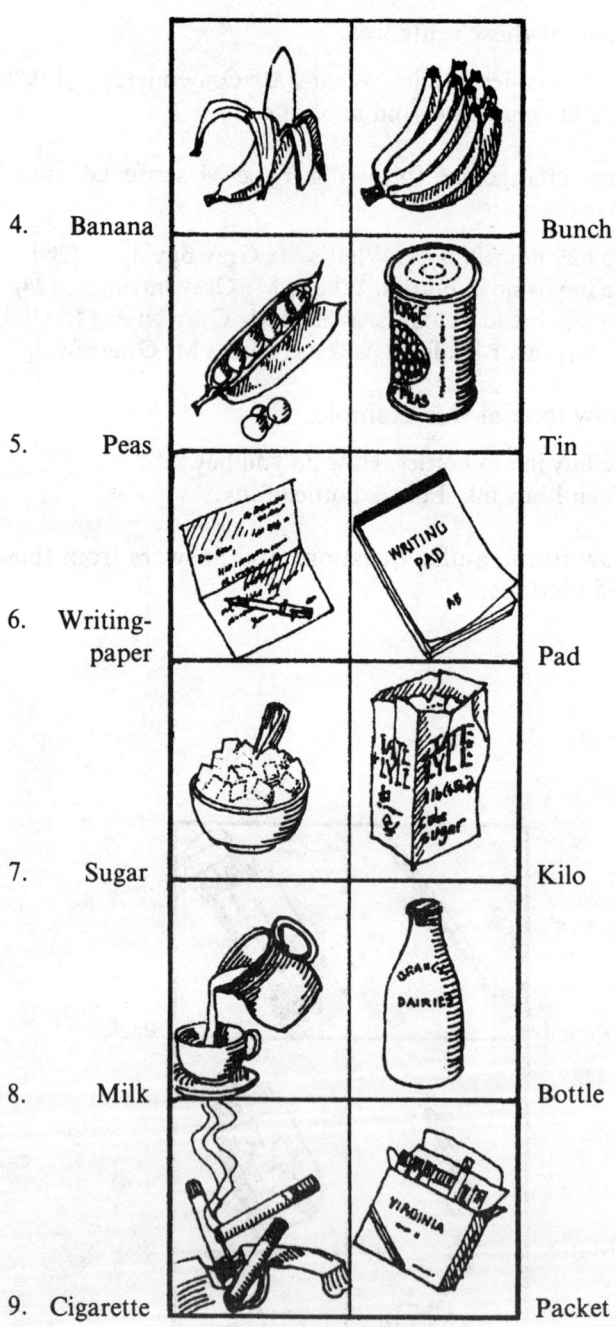

4.	Banana	Bunch
5.	Peas	Tin
6.	Writing-paper	Pad
7.	Sugar	Kilo
8.	Milk	Bottle
9.	Cigarette	Packet

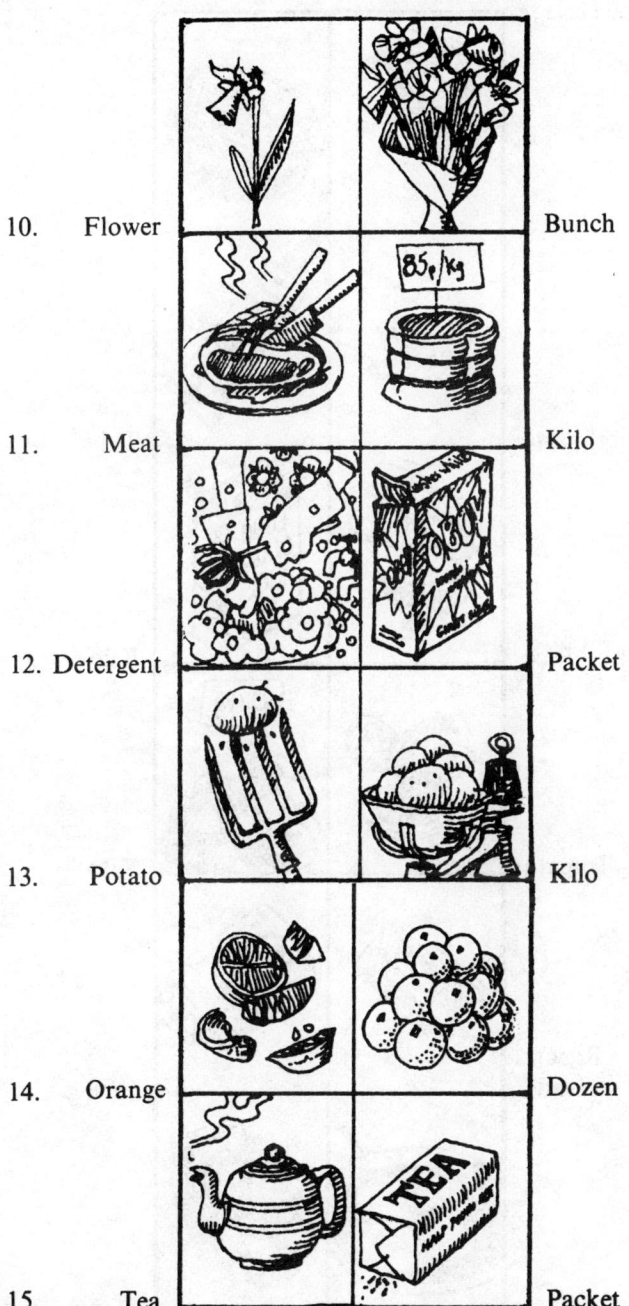

10. Flower	Bunch
11. Meat	Kilo
12. Detergent	Packet
13. Potato	Kilo
14. Orange	Dozen
15. Tea	Packet

33

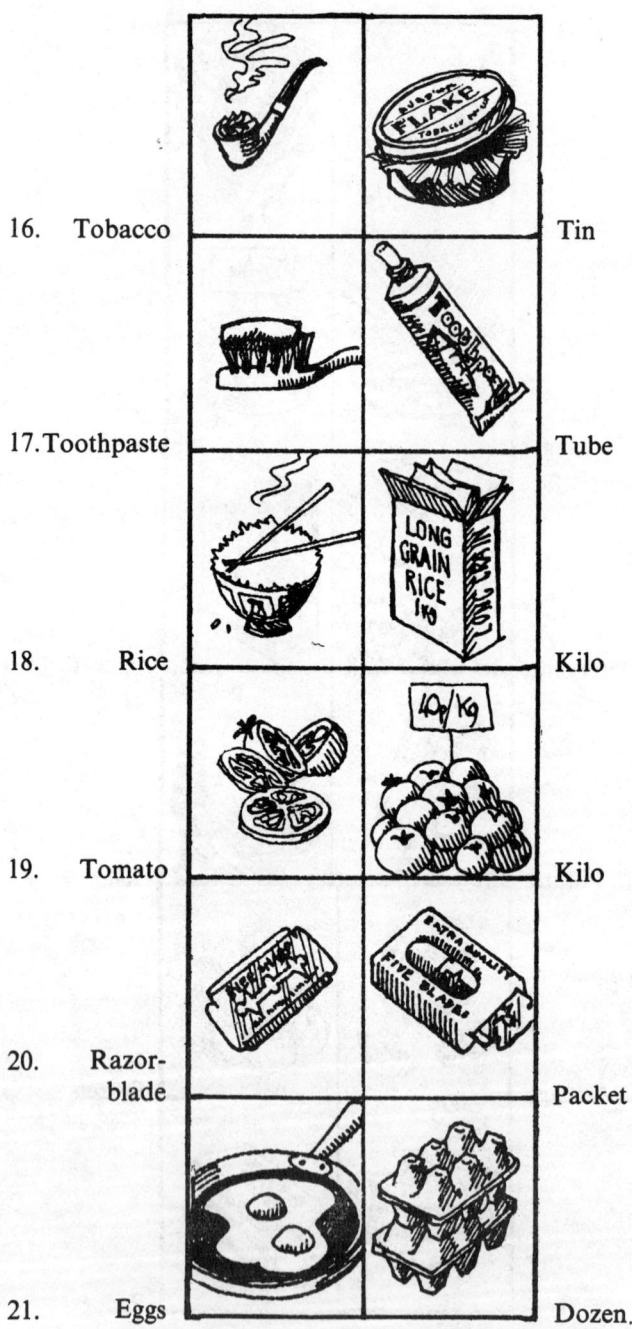

16. Tobacco   Tin

17. Toothpaste   Tube

18. Rice   Kilo

19. Tomato   Kilo

20. Razor-blade   Packet

21. Eggs   Dozen.

A salesman is visiting Mr Gray. He wants to
sell a lot of goods. Here is their conversation.

'Good afternoon, Mr
Gray. How are you?'

'Good afternoon, Mr
Wheeler, I'm well,
thanks. How are you?'

'Fine thank you.'

'Please sit down.'

'Thank you. Do you sell
much coffee?'

'Yes, I sell a lot of coffee.'

'You don't buy much
from us.'

'Oh, yes I do. I buy a lot.'

'You haven't got much
on the shelves.'

'No, but I've got a lot
in the warehouse.'

'Cigarette? Do you
smoke many cigarettes?'

'Yes, I smoke a lot.
I smoke twenty
cigarettes a day.'

'I don't smoke much.
I smoke very few
cigarettes a day. Light?'

Thank you. Well now,
let's get down to
business. I want to order
a lot of goods from you.'

Language Points

Look at these sentences.

Do you sell *much* coffee?

Yes, I sell *a lot of* coffee.

You haven't got *much* on the shelves.

No, but I've got *a lot* in the warehouse.

Do you smoke *many* cigarettes?

Yes, I smoke *a lot*.

In affirmative sentences we usually use *a lot (of)*.
In negative sentences and in questions we usually use
    much with singular nouns.
    many with plural nouns.

Exercise V

Look at these sentences.

Type A   Miss Brown doesn't eat much.
Type B.   Oh, yes, she does. She eats a lot.

Type A.   John doesn't type many letters.
Type B.   Oh, yes he does. He types a lot.

Give Type B responses to these Type A sentences.

1. The salesman doesn't smoke much.
2. There aren't many goods in the warehouse.
3. The waiter isn't bringing many chips for you.
4. That Brazilian doesn't drink much coffee.
5. The baby doesn't want much milk.
6. Caroline doesn't buy much meat at the butcher's.
7. There aren't many pictures in our office.
8. He isn't introducing many people to us.

Look at these sentences

Mr Gray doesn't sell much detergent.

He sells *very little* detergent.

The salesman doesn't smoke many cigarettes a day.

He smokes *very few* cigarettes.

36

Exercise W   Look at these sentences.

Type I.   John eats a lot.
Type J.   Oh, no, he doesn't. He doesn't eat much. He eats very little.
Type I.   Miss Brown types a lot of letters.
Type J.   Oh, no, she doesn't. She doesn't type many. She types very few.

Give Type J responses to these Type I sentences.

1.   The grocer sells a lot of tomatoes.
2.   There's a lot of money in the safe.
3.   Caroline drinks a lot of coffee.
4.   Mrs Dean is buying a lot of potatoes.
5.   There are a lot of people in this room.
6.   There's a lot of tea in that packet.
7.   He's got a lot of books.
8.   That Swede has got a lot of children.
9.   The baby's got a lot of teeth.
10. Mr Dean dictates a lot of letters.

What time is it?

It's ten o'clock.

It's half-past three.

It's a quarter-past five.

It's a quarter to six.

What time is it now?

What time is it now?

Exercise X   What time is it?

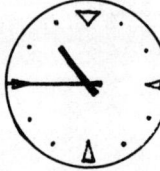

Exercise Y   Answer these questions.

1. At what time do you get up every morning?
2. At what time do you have breakfast?
3. What time is it now?
4. At what time do you come to class?

Look at Lesson Six.

5. At what time does Mr Williams get up?
6. At what time does he leave the hotel?
7. At what time does the manager arrive?
8. At what time do you leave the house every morning?
9. At what time do you have lunch?
10. At what time does the grocer's open every morning?

Telling the Time
Look at these clocks:

When it's twelve o'clock, we say:

In the daytime:
It's midday.
It's noon.
It's twelve p.m.
It's twelve hundred hours.

At night-time:
It's midnight.
It's twelve a.m.
It's twenty-four hundred hours.

In the morning we say:
It's twenty-five minutes to ten in the morning.
It's 9.35 (nine thirty-five) a.m.
It's 09.35 (o-nine thirty-five) hours.

In the evening we say:
It's twenty-five minutes to ten in the evening.
It's 9.35 (nine thirty-five) p.m.
It's 21.35 (twenty-one thirty-five) hours.

In the morning we say:
It's a quarter past two.
It's 2.15 (two fifteen) a.m.
It's 02.15 (o-two fifteen) hours.

In the afternoon we say:
It's quarter past two in the afternoon.
It's 2.15 (two fifteen) p.m.
It's 14.15 (fourteen fifteen) hours.

In the morning we say:
It's ten minutes past eight in the morning.
It's 8.10 (eight ten) a.m.
It's 08.10 (o-eight ten) hours.

In the evening we say:
It's ten minutes past eight in the evening.
It's 8.10 (eight ten) p.m.
It's 20.10 (twenty ten) hours.

Exercise Z   Look at these examples.

7.20 a.m.

Mr Davis says to his wife:	It's twenty minutes past seven in the morning.
Mr Davis says to his secretary:	My train leaves at 7.20 (seven-twenty) a.m.
Mr Johnson says:	The plane arrives in Zurich at 07.20 (o-seven twenty) hours.

4.55 p.m.

Mr Davis says to his wife:	It's five minutes to five in the afternoon.
Mr Davis says to his secretary:	My train leaves at 4.55 (four fifty-five) p.m.
Mr Johnson says:	The plane arrives in Zurich at 16.55 (sixteen fifty-five) hours.

Now in each of the following cases:
What does Mr Davis say to his wife?
What does Mr Davis say to his secretary?
What does Mr Johnson say?

3.15 a.m.	7.35 p.m.	10.25 p.m.	6.45 p.m.
4.30 a.m.	4.35 a.m.	9.00 a.m.	11.20 p.m.
12.00 p.m.	6.10 a.m.	8.50 p.m.	12.55 p.m.
2.05 a.m.	1.45 p.m.	10.00 p.m.	8.40 a.m.

Jean and Caroline are travelling on a bus.

Jean: Caroline, look there's something on the floor.

Caroline: Oh, yes, what is it?

Jean: Goodness! Two airline tickets to Rome.

Caroline: Whose are they?

Jean: Let's ask these people in front. Excuse me. Are these tickets yours?

Man: No, they're not ours.

Jean: Let's ask that man over there. Perhaps they're his. Excuse me, are these tickets yours?

Man: No, they're not mine.

Jean: Let's ask the lady behind. Perhaps they're hers. Excuse me, are these tickets yours?

Lady: Let me see. Heavens they're mine. Thank you very much.

Exercise 100   (one hundred)

1.	The tickets don't belong to Caroline.	They're not hers.
2.	They don't belong to the people in front.	They're not theirs.
3.	They don't belong to the man.	They're not his.
4.	They belong to the lady behind.	They're hers.
5.	This book doesn't belong to you.	It's not yours.

6. It belongs to me. It's mine.
7. These pens belong to us. They're ours.
8. Does this typewriter belong to you? Is it yours?
9. Does this packet of cigarettes belong to John? Is it his?
10. Do these spectacles belong to you? Are they yours?

Exercise 101   (one hundred and one)

Look at these sentences.

Whose car is this? (my)
It's my car.   It belongs to me.   It's mine.

Whose files are these?   (their)
They're their files.   They belong to them.   They're theirs.

Now give three responses to these sentences in the same way.

1. Whose pair of scissors is this? (your)
2. Whose tube of toothpaste is this?   (his)
3. Whose radio is this?   (their)
4. Whose pens are these?   (their)
5. Whose picture is this?   (our)
6. Whose bags of sugar are these?   (my)
7. Whose chair is this?   (your)
8. Whose books are these?   (our)
9. Whose office is this?   (his)
10. Whose bicycle is this?   (her)

Exercise 102   (one hundred and two)

Listen to your teacher.

This is a newsagent's
shop.
Whose is it?

It's Mr Turner's.

What does he sell?

He sells newspapers and
magazines.

This is Mrs Turner.
Who is she?

She's Mr Turner's wife.

Mrs Turner finds a
handbag in the shop.
She says: 'Who does
this belong to?'

Mr Turner says:
'It's Mrs Dean's. She
forgets it every time.'

What magazines and
newspapers does
Mr Turner sell?
He sells 'Boy'.

It's a boys' magazine.

He sells 'Business News',
too.

It's a businessmen's
newspaper.

He sells 'Fashion', as well.

It's a women's magazine.

Mrs Turner says: 'Whose bicycle is that on the pavement?'

Mr Turner says: 'It's John's.'

Mrs Turner says: 'No, it's not . . .'

It's a girl's bicycle.

Exercise 110   (one hundred and ten)
Look at these examples.

Type J.   This magazine is not for girls.
Type K.   It's not a girls' magazine.

Type J.   These cups belong to Mrs Turner.
Type K.   They're Mrs Turner's cups.

Now turn these Type J sentences into Type K sentences.

1.   This tin of tobacco belongs to that man.
2.   This magazine is for men.
3.   These books don't belong to the secretaries.
4.   This office is for the managers.
5.   This shop belongs to the butcher.
6.   That car belongs to Mr Dean.
7.   This toothpaste is not for children.
8.   That money is not for the office-boy.
9.   These cigarettes belong to John.
10.   That banana is for Caroline.

Exercise 111   (one hundred and eleven)
Listen to your teacher.

Mr Dean is the Managing Director of the Wickham Engineering
Company. Miss Jean Brown is his secretary.

What does Miss Brown
do every morning?

What did she do this
morning?

She arrives at the office
at nine o'clock.

She arrived at the office
at nine.

She opens the
correspondence.

She opened the
correspondence.

She places the letters
on Mr Dean's desk.

She placed the letters
on Mr Dean's desk.

She talks to the
office-boy.

She talked to the
office-boy.

What does Mr Dean do
every morning?

What did he do this
morning?

He arrives at the office
at half-past nine.

He arrived there at
half-past nine this
morning.

He asks Miss Brown:
'Is there much mail?'

He asked her:
'Is there much mail?'

He looks at the
correspondence.

He looked at the
correspondence.

He dictates some letters
to Miss Brown.

He dictated some letters
to Miss Brown.

He orders a cup of
coffee.

He ordered a cup of
coffee at eleven.

He smokes his pipe.

He smoked his pipe.

Exercise 124 (one hundred and twenty-four)

Look at these sentences.

Type R.   Mr Dean smokes his pipe every day.
Type S.   He smoked it yesterday.
Type T.   He didn't smoke it last Wednesday.

Now make Type S and Type T sentences from these Type R sentences.

1. She asks a lot of questions every day.
2. You answer the telephone every day.
3. They type some correspondence every day.
4. We order a cup of coffee every day.
5. I sign a lot of letters every day.
6. You look for your pen every day.
7. That Greek talks to me every day.
8. We listen to the radio every day.
9. The office boy arrives at the office at 8.30 every day.
10. You wait for the bus every day.

Exercise 135   (one hundred and thirty-five)

Look at these sentences.

Mr Dean smokes his pipe every day.

Did he smoke it this morning?
Yes, he did.

Now respond to the sentences in Exercise 124 in the same way.

Exercise 147   (one hundred and forty-seven)

Look at these sentences.

Mr Dean smoked his pipe this afternoon.
Oh, no he didn't. He didn't smoke it this afternoon.

Now respond to these sentences in the same way.

1. She asked a lot of questions this afternoon.
2. You answered the telephone this afternoon.
3. They typed some correspondence this afternoon.
4. We ordered a cup of tea this afternoon.
5. I signed a lot of letters this afternoon.
6. You looked for your pen this afternoon.
7. That Greek talked to me this afternoon.
8. We listened to the radio this afternoon.
9. John arrived at the office at 2.30 this afternoon.
10. You waited for the bus this afternoon.

What happens every evening?

What happened yesterday evening?

Every evening Mr Dean leaves the office at half-past five, and goes to the station.

Yesterday evening Mr Dean left the office at half-past five and went to the station.

He buys a newspaper and goes into the bar.

He bought a newspaper and went into the bar.

He says: 'Good evening,' to the barman.

He said 'Good evening,' to the barman.

The barman brings him a glass of beer and puts it on the counter. Mr Dean pays for it and drinks it.

The barman brought him a glass of beer and put it on the counter. Mr Dean paid for it and drank it.

Then he goes and gets on the train. After twenty minutes, Mr Dean gets off the train.

Then he went and got on the train. After twenty minutes Mr Dean got off the train.

Mrs Dean meets him and takes him home in the car.

Mrs Dean met him and took him home in the car.

Exercise 158   (one hundred and fifty-eight)

Answer these questions.

1. What time did Mr Dean leave the office?
2. Where did he go?
3. What did he buy first?
4. Where did he go next?
5. What did he say to the barman?
6. What did the barman bring?
7. What did Mr Dean do before drinking the beer?
8. What did he do after paying for the beer?
9. Where did he go after drinking the beer?
10. What did he do after twenty minutes?
11. What did Mrs Dean do?   (She did two things.)

Exercise 182 (one hundred and eighty-two)

Look at these sentences.

Type G. Did you drink that cup of tea? (drank)
Type H. Yes, I did. I drank it just now.

Now make Type H sentences from these Type G sentences.

1.	Did you write that letter?	(wrote)
2.	Did you do that exercise?	(did)
3.	Did you eat those cakes?	(ate)
4.	Did you give that book to my friend?	(gave)
5.	Did you come into the office?	(came)
7.	Did you pay for the coffee?	(paid)
8.	Did you buy the flour?	(bought)
9.	Did you take my pen?	(took)
10.	Did you sit on that chair?	(sat)
11.	Did you stand at the window?	(stood)
12.	Did you bring that file?	(brought)

Exercise 199 (one hundred and ninety-nine)

Look at these sentences and pictures.

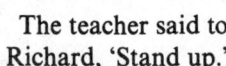

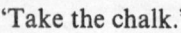

The teacher said to
Richard, 'Stand up.'   Richard stood up.

'Come to the
blackboard.'   He came to the
blackboard.

'Take the chalk.'   He took the chalk.

'Write your name.'   He wrote his name.

'Go back to your place.'   He went back to his
                                      place.

'Sit down.'   He sat down.

Now do the same as Richard. What did you do?

Conversation   Look at this conversation between Mrs Davis and Mrs Collins.

Mrs Davis: My husband and I were at the Odeon Cinema last night. There were a lot of people. *Were you there?* We didn't see you.

Mrs Collins: Oh, yes, *I was there*. I saw you. My *husband wasn't there,* but my sister went with me. Did you like the film?

Mrs Davis: No, we didn't. My brother and his friend saw it last Thursday. They liked the beginning but not the end.

Mrs Collins: It wasn't a very good film. We left before the end.

Mrs Davis: At the end there wasn't anybody in the cinema except us. It was a very bad film.

Mrs Collins: Well, nice to see you, Mrs Davis.

Mrs Davis: And you. Goodbye, Mrs Collins.

Mrs Collins: Goodbye, Mrs Davis.

Language Points   Notice that in English we say:

I was there.   (I was ....)
Were you there?   (You were ....)
My husband wasn't there.   (He was ....)
My husband and I were at the Odeon   (We were ....)
                                            and also ....   (They were)
There wasn't anybody in the cinema   (There was ....)
There were a lot of people.   (There were ....)

Exercise 204   (two hundred and four)

Put 'was' or 'were' into these sentences.

1.   .... it a good film?
2.   There .... (not) many people in the cinema.

3. Jean and Caroline .... at the florist's.
4. John and Miss Brown .... (not) at the office this morning.
5. Mr Johnson's brother .... there.
6. There .... a book on the table.
7. He .... Brazilian, but his wife .... Swedish.
8. I .... at the grocer's this morning.
9. That .... (not) the beginning of the film. It .... the end.
10. .... (not we) in London yesterday?

Exercise 264 (two hundred and sixty-four)

Look at these sentences.

Was that your sister? Yes, it was.
Weren't we here last week? Yes, we were.
Were you a teacher? No, I wasn't.

Now answer these questions in the same way.

1. Was Mrs Davis with Mr Davis at the cinema?
2. Was Mr Collins there?
3. Was Mrs Collins there?
4. Was it a good film?
5. Was Mrs Collins's sister there?
6. Were there many people in the cinema at the beginning?
7. Was there anybody except Mr and Mrs Davis in the cinema at the end of the film?
8. Was it a bad film?
9. Were Mrs Davis's brother and his friend at the Odeon last Friday?

Exercise 287 (two hundred and eighty-seven)

Answer these questions about the conversation.

1. Who did Mrs Davis go to the cinema with?
2. Did she see Mrs Collins there?
3. Was Mr Collins with his wife?
4. Did Mrs Collins see anybody at the cinema? Who did she see?
5. Did Mr and Mrs Davis like the film?
6. Who was Mrs Davis's brother with?
7. Did Mrs Davis's brother and his friend like the end of the film?
8. What did Mrs Collins and her sister do before the end?
9. Was the cinema crowded at the end of the film?
10. What did Mrs Collins say to Mrs Davis at the end of the conversation?

Exercise 301 (three hundred and one)

Listen to your teacher.

When John was on holiday, he wrote to his uncle. Here is the letter.

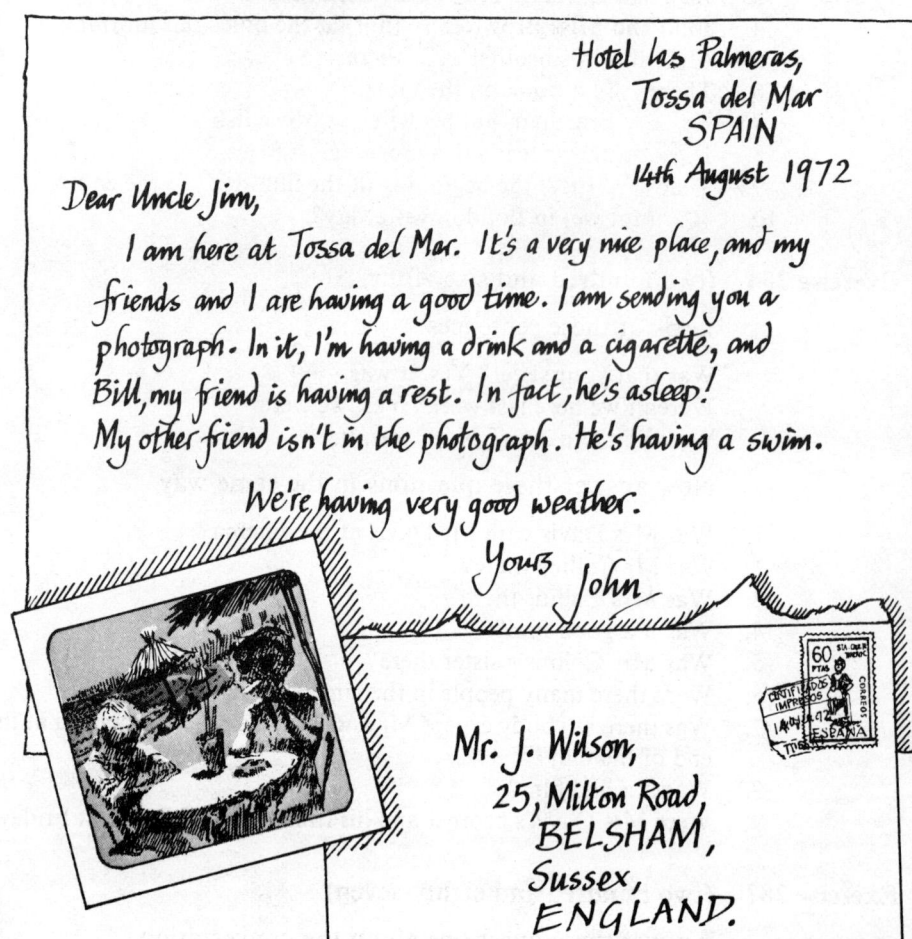

> Hotel las Palmeras,
> Tossa del Mar
> SPAIN
> 14th August 1972
>
> Dear Uncle Jim,
> I am here at Tossa del Mar. It's a very nice place, and my friends and I are having a good time. I am sending you a photograph. In it, I'm having a drink and a cigarette, and Bill, my friend is having a rest. In fact, he's asleep! My other friend isn't in the photograph. He's having a swim.
> We're having very good weather.
>
> Yours John

> Mr. J. Wilson,
> 25, Milton Road,
> BELSHAM,
> Sussex,
> ENGLAND.

Here is the photograph.   Here is the envelope.

Reading
Language   Look at these sentences in John's letter.
Points

My friends and I *are having* a good time.
I'*m having* a drink and a cigarette.
Bill, my friend, *is having* a rest.
He'*s having* a swim.
We'*re having* very good weather.

Exercise 347 (three hundred and forty-seven)

On 17th August 1973, John's friend Bill wrote a letter to his mother from Tossa de Mar. He sent this photograph.

Have a look at the photograph, and then answer the questions in this exercise. Then write Bill's letter. Begin 'Dear Mother' and end 'Love . . . Bill'.

1. Bill, where are you?
2. What's Tossa de Mar like? (It's . . . .)
3. Do you and your friends like Tossa de Mar? (My friends and I are having . . . .)
5. Are you sending anything? (I'm . . . .)
6. What are you doing in the photograph?
7. What's John doing? (John . . . .)
8. What's David doing? (David . . . .)
9. What sort of weather are you having? (We . . . .)

Exercise 356   (three hundred and fifty-six)

Have a good look at these pictures.

What are Mrs Turner and Mrs Dean doing?   They're having coffee.

What did John do at half-past seven this morning?   He had breakfast.

What did Miss Brown
do at a quarter to one?

She had lunch.

What are Mr and Mrs
Dean doing in this
picture?

They're having dinner.

What's Tommy doing?

He's having a bath.

What's David doing?

He's having a shower.

What are Mrs Davis and
Mrs Collins doing?

They're having a talk.

Exercise 361   (three hundred and sixty-one)

Put the correct form of the verb 'have' in the sentences below.

am having
is having
are having
had
or the negative

1. I .... a talk with my sister yesterday.
2. He (not) .... a bath this morning.
3. In the first photograph, Bill .... a good rest.
4. John .... dinner now.
5. Mr Dean .... a beer at the station yesterday.
6. At the moment .... a look at this picture.
7. I (not) .... breakfast this morning.
8. John, David and Bill are in Spain. ? .... ? a good time?
9. Where .... (he) .... lunch?
10. You (not) .... a shower this morning.

Exercise 400   (four hundred)

Look at these sentences.

Type G.   Tommy's having a bath.   (every day)   (yesterday)
Type H.   Is he?
Type I.   Yes, he has a bath every day.
Type J.   He doesn't. He didn't have a bath yesterday.

Give Type H, I, and J sentences for each of these Type G sentences.

1. Mr Dean's having a beer.   (every evening)   (yesterday)
2. John and Bill are having a good time in Spain.   (every year)
                                                        (last year)
3. John's having breakfast.   (every day)   (yesterday)
4. Jean and Caroline are having coffee.   (every Friday)
                                             (last Friday)
5. David's having a rest.   (every day)   (last Tuesday)
6. Miss Brown's having lunch.   (at a quarter to one every day)
                                                (at all yesterday)
7. Mr Johnson's having a cigarette.   (after lunch every day)
                                          (after lunch last Sunday)
8. Tommy's having an ice-cream.   (every afternoon)
                                     (yesterday afternoon)
9. David's having a swim.   (before lunch every day)
                               (at all last Sunday)
10. Mr and Mrs Dean are having dinner.   (at eight o'clock every
                                evening)   (at all last Wednesday)

Last January Mr Jones was in Rio de Janeiro.

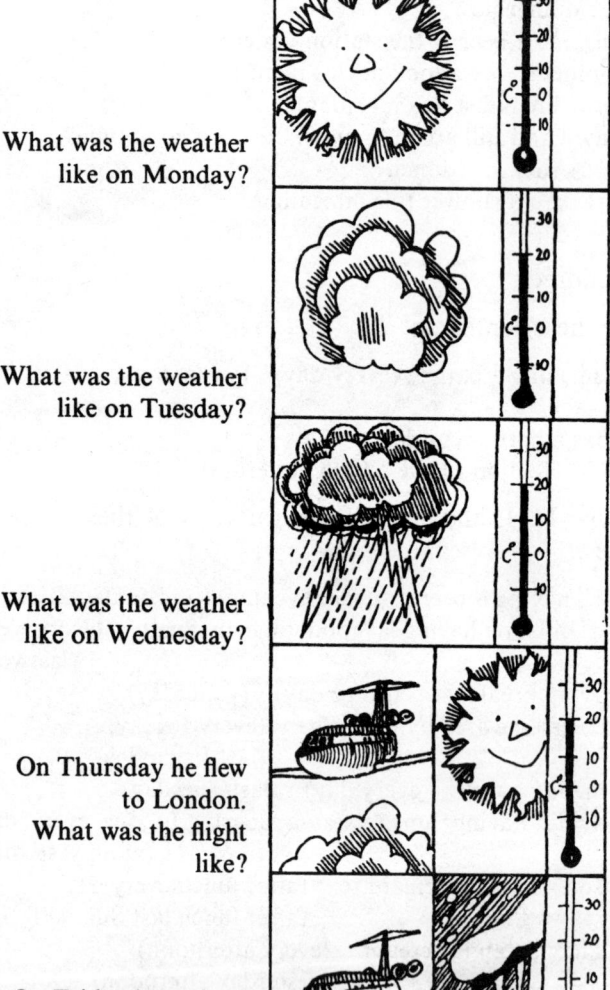

What was the weather like on Monday?

It was good. The sun shone. It was hot.

What was the weather like on Tuesday?

It was cloudy, but it was warm. It didn't rain.

What was the weather like on Wednesday?

It was bad. There was a thunderstorm. It wasn't cold.

On Thursday he flew to London. What was the flight like?

The flight was good.

On Friday he arrived in London. What was the weather like?

It was bad. It snowed. It was very cold.

Names of the months
Learn the names of the months in English.

January, February, March, April, May, June, July, August, September, October, November, December.

Exercise 410 (four hundred and ten)

Answer these questions.

1. What's the weather like today?
2. What was it like yesterday?
3. What was it like last Saturday?
4. What was it like last Sunday?
5. What's the weather like here in January?
6. What's it like in March?
7. What's it like in June?
8. What's it like in September?
9. Do you like hot weather?
10. Do you like cold weather?

What are they like?

On the left you see Jean.

Jean's tall.
Jean's thin.
Jean's fair.
Jean's got blue eyes.
Jean's good-looking.

On the right you see Paul.

Paul's short.
Paul's fat.
Paul's dark.
Paul's got brown eyes.
Paul's ugly.

Exercise 411 (four hundred and eleven)

Listen to your teacher.

Test for Lessons Eleven to Twenty

Exercise A   Read this passage.

In August every year I visit Spain. I travel by train and stay at a hotel near the beach. When I arrive I have a shower, and then I go to the bar. The barman knows me and gives me a glass of beer. In the daytime there aren't many people in the bar, but every evening a lot of French people come there. They buy drinks for me and I have a good time.

Now write this passage again as a letter.

Your address is:
31, Green Street,
Boreham,
Norfolk

Write to your Uncle Jim and say what happened. Do not write, 'In August every year' at the beginning. Write 'In August'. You write the letter on 14th October, 1973. At the end write 'Yours' and sign the letter.

Exercise B   Look at these sentences.

Type S.   This bicycle belongs to my brother.
Type T.   It's my brother's bicycle.

Now turn these Type S sentences into Type T sentences.

1. This magazine is for salesmen.
2. This bottle of wine belongs to that lady.
3. That ice-cream is for my husband.
4. That shop belongs to those Frenchmen.
5. This pair of spectacles belongs to my neighbour.

Exercise C   Look at these sentences.

Type U.   Does this pipe belong to you?
Type V.   Is it yours?

Now turn these Type U questions into Type V questions.

1. Do these bananas belong to you?
2. Does this airline-ticket belong to your sister?
3. Do these bags belong to those Brazilians?
4. Does this packet of detergent belong to me?
5. Are these headphones for us?
6. Does this warehouse belong to the grocer?

60

Exercise D   Look at these sentences.

Type W.   John ate a lot.
Type X.   Oh, no, he didn't. He didn't eat much. He ate very little.

Type W.   Miss Brown typed a lot of letters.
Type X.   Oh, no, she didn't. She didn't type many. She typed very few.

Now turn these Type W sentences into Type X sentences.

1.   Mr Dean drank a lot of beer.
2.   Your brother went to a lot of films in October.
3.   These women's fashion-magazines had got a lot of pictures.
4.   I ate a lot of ice-creams.
5.   That airline flew a lot of planes.
6.   In Spain we had a lot of bad weather.

Exercise E   Look at these sentences.

        7.20 a.m.

Mr Davis says to his wife: It's twenty minutes past seven in the morning.
Mr Dean says to his secretary: The plane leaves at o-seven twenty hours.

What do Mr Davis and Mr Dean say here?
1.   14.55
2.   3.45
3.   12.20

Exercise F   Read this passage.

This evening, Mr Davis got on a bus and went to the cinema. He saw a film. Then he had dinner.

Now write the passage again, beginning 'Every evening, Mr Davis gets on . . .'

Vocabulary introduced in Lessons 11 to 20

address			
afternoon	asleep	banana	beer
afterwards	at once	bar (of soap)	beginning
airline	August	bar (for drinks)	belong
a.m.	bad	barman	between
April	bag	beach	blue

bottle	florist	March	see
box	fly	match	send
bread	forget	May	September
break	friend	midday	shelf
brother	gentleman	midnight	short
brown	get off	milk	shower (bath)
bunch	get on	mine	shine (v)
bus	glass	minute	sister
businessman	go back	morning	smoke (v)
cake	good	much	show
car	good-looking	news	snow
chalk	Goodness!	newsagent	soap
cinema	goods	newspaper	sort
class	good time (have a)	nice	station
clock	grocer	nighttime	stock
cloudy	happen	noon	sun
cold	Heavens!	November	swim (have a)
company	here	October	talk (n)
conversation	hers	open (adj)	tall
correspondence	his	orange	tea
crowded	(on) holiday	other	Thank you very
dark	hot	ours	much
day	hotel	passage	theirs
daytime	hour	past (half past one	thin
December	husband	etc.)	thing
detergent	ice-cream	pavement	thunderstorm
dinner	in fact	pea	tin
dozen	ink	photograph	tobacco
drink (n)	It doesn't matter	pipe (for smoking)	tomato
egg	January	place (v)	toothpaste
end	July	plane	train
evening	June	potato	travel (v)
every morning	kilo	pound	tube
Excuse me	lady	p.m.	ugly
exercise	let's get down to	(a) quarter past	uncle
eye	business	(a) quarter to	visit
fair	let me see	question	warehouse
fashion	light?	radio	warm
February	like (v)	rain (v)	weather
few	little	razor-blade	wholesaler
film	loaf	rest (have a)	wine
flight	(a) lot of	rice	writing-paper
Fine, thank you	managing director	Rio de Janeiro	yesterday
floor	magazine	room	yours
flour	mail	salesman	Zurich
flower	many	same	

62

Conversation

Mr Dean is entertaining Monsieur Dupré, a Belgian business-friend, at a restaurant.

Mr Dean: Here we are. Where would you like to sit?

Monsieur Dupré: I'd like to sit here. I like the view from the window.

Waiter: Would you like a drink before lunch, Sir?

Mr Dean: No, thank you, not for me. Monsieur Dupré, would you like a drink?

Monsieur Dupré: No, thank you, not just now. I'm afraid I don't like to drink at lunch.

Mr Dean: Would you like to start with some soup?

Monsieur Dupré: Yes, please, I would. I like soup for lunch and at dinner.

Mr Dean (to the waiter):   My friend would like some soup.

Waiter: Certainly, Sir. Would you like some soup, too, Sir?

Mr Dean: Yes, I'd like some soup. Monsieur Dupré, would you like a steak after the soup?

Monsieur Dupré: Yes, please, I would. I like steak very much.

Language Points   Look at the dialogue carefully. Notice that these sentences occur:

Type A: Where *would you like* to sit?
I*'d like* to sit here.
Would you like a drink?
Would you like to start with soup?
Yes, please, I would.
My friend *would like* some soup.

Would you like some soup too?
Yes, *I'd like* some soup.
Would you like a steak after the soup.
Yes, please, I would.

Type B: *I like* the view from the window.
I'm afraid I don't like to drink at lunch.
I like soup for lunch and dinner.
I like steak very much.

We use Type A sentences when we would or would not like something *now*.
We use Type B sentences when we like or do not like something *in general*.

Notice too, that we say *at* lunch, *at* dinner, *for* lunch, *for* dinner, and also *at* breakfast, *at* tea, *for* breakfast, *for* tea.

Exercise 475 (four hundred and seventy-five)

Look at these examples.
Would you like a drink? Yes, please, I would.
Would you like some soup? Yes, please, I would.
BUT
Would you like some coffee? *No, thank you, not just now.*
Would you like a cake? *No, thank you, not just now.*

We don't say: No, I wouldn't.

Now complete these sentences.

1. Would you like a cup of tea? No, ...
2. Would you like to sit here? Yes, ...
3. Would you like breakfast now? Yes, ...
4. Would you like an orange? No, ...
5. Would you like some wine? Yes, ...
6. Would you like some eggs? Yes, ...
7. Would you like a cigarette? No, ...
8. Would you like some bread? No, ...

Notice that we say:

Would you like *some* eggs?
                some wine?   (not *any*)

Exercise 484 (four hundred and eighty-four)

Now look at these sentences.

Do you like these flowers? *Yes, I do.*
Do you like eggs? *No, I'm afraid I don't.*
Do you like sugar in coffee? *No, I'm afraid I don't.*

Notice that we don't say: No, I don't.

Now complete these sentences.

1. Do you like this tobacco? No, ...
2. Do you like soup at dinner? Yes, ...
3. Do you like steak? No, ...
4. Do you like to drink at lunch? No, ...
5. Do you like cakes? Yes, ...
6. Do you like wine for dinner? Yes, ...
7. Do you like to listen to the radio? Yes, ...
8. Do you like this shop? No, ...

Exercise 502   (five hundred and two)

Notice that we also say:

Do you like these flowers. *Yes, I like them very much.*
                          (not a LOT)
Do you like eggs? *No, I'm afraid I don't like them at all.*
Do you like sugar? *No, I'm afraid I don't like it at all.*

Do the sentences in Exercise 484 again, using these expressions.

One day, in Spain, David went into a bank.

David said to the
clerk behind the counter:

The clerk said:

'Excuse me. Can you
speak English?'

'Yes, I can. I can speak
it a little.'

'Can you understand
me?'

'Yes, I can.'

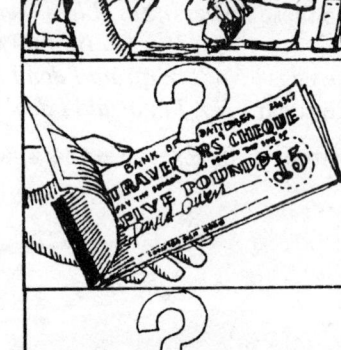

'Can you change these
cheques?'

'Yes, we can.'

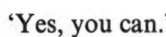

'Can I sign the cheques
then?'

'Yes, you can.'

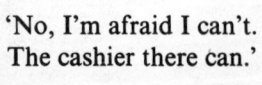

'Can you give me the
money?'

'No, I'm afraid I can't.
The cashier there can.'

David went to the
cashier and said:
'Excuse me. Can you
speak English?'

The man said nothing.
He couldn't speak
English.

David couldn't speak Spanish, but the man could understand and gave him the money.

Exercise 612 (six hundred and twelve)

Notice the answers to these questions.

'*Can you* speak English?' '*Yes, I can.*'
'*Can you* change these cheques?' '*Yes, we can.*'
'*Can I* sign the cheques, then?' '*Yes, you can.*'
'*Can you* give me the money then?' 'No, *I'm afraid I can't.*'

Now answer these questions.

1. Can you speak English?
2. Can the teacher speak English?
3. Can you swim?
4. Can you type?
5. Can the students in this class speak Swedish?
6. Can we buy meat at a butcher's?

Exercise 615 (six hundred and fifteen)

Look at the conversations in the bank again. Say what happened. Answer the questions with *Could* or *Couldn't*.

1. Could the clerk speak English?
2. Could he understand David?
3. Could the people in the bank change David's cheques?
4. Could David sign the cheques?
5. Could the clerk give David the money?
6. Who could give him the money?
7. Could the other man speak English?
8. Could David speak Spanish?
9. Could the cashier understand?
10. Could he give David the money?

Exercise 640 (six hundred and forty)

Look at these sentences.

Type C. The man gave *David the money.*
Type D. The man gave *the money to David.*

Now change these Type C sentences into Type D sentences.

1. Mr Dean gave his wife a car last month.
2. Did the chemist give you that tube of toothpaste?
3. Please give me that cheque.
4. Give him a dozen eggs.
5. My sister gives them a lot of potatoes for lunch.
6. In the picture Bill is giving John a cigarette.
7. Did you give him a cup of tea?
8. Did you give him that letter?
9. He didn't give us any flowers.
10. Can you give her your pad and your pencil?

Today Mr Dean is leaving the office on business. Yesterday, he said these things to Miss Brown.

'Miss Brown, please type these letters tomorrow.'

He asked her to type some letters.

'Please pay the cleaning-woman.'

He asked her to pay the cleaning woman.

'Please buy some pens.'

He asked her to buy some pens.

'Please telephone Mr Johnson.'

He asked her to telephone Mr Johnson.

He said these things to John.

'Take these letters to the post-office.'

He told John to take some letters to the post-office.

'Clean the typewriter.'

He told John to clean the typewriter.

69

'Don't arrive late.' He told John not to arrive late.

'Don't leave early.' He told John not to leave early.

Exercise 754 (seven hundred and fifty-four)

Now study the sentences and pictures above. Then cover up the sentences on the right, and answer these questions.

What did Mr Dean ask Miss Brown to do?
What did he tell John to do?

Exercise 898 (eight hundred and ninety-eight)

Look at these sentences.

Type E. 'Drink your coffee,' she said to me.
Type F. 'She told me to drink my coffee.'

Type E. 'Please don't go to the cinema,' my husband said to me.
Type F. 'My husband asked me not to go to the cinema.'

Now change these Type E sentences into Type F sentences.

1. 'Please buy some bananas at the greengrocer's,' my wife said to me.
2. 'Don't give him the car,' my friend said to her.
3. 'Please open the safe,' said the manager to the office-boy.
4. 'Put some ink in your pen,' the secretary said to you.
5. 'Give me a piece of chalk, please,' said the teacher to the student.
6. 'Please don't eat many cakes,' Jean said to Caroline.
7. 'Please don't listen to the radio,' said John to David.
8. 'Don't wait for the bus,' the boy said to his friend.
9. 'Change the cheques, please,' said the Frenchman to the bank-clerk.
10. 'Don't smoke the cigarette,' he said to me.

Exercise 1,177 (one thousand, one hundred and seventy-seven)

Look at Exercise 199, Lesson Seventeen, on page 50, and listen to the teacher.

Mr Dean is away on business.
Miss Brown must do these things:

She must type some
letters.

What must she do first?

She must pay the
cleaning-woman.

Who must she pay?

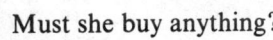

She must buy
some pens.

Must she buy anything?

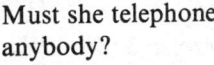

She must telephone
Mr Johnson.

Must she telephone
anybody?

John must do these things:

He must take some
letters to the
post-office.

What must he do first?

He must clean the
typewriter.

Must he clean anything?

He mustn't do these things:

He mustn't arrive late.

What mustn't he do?

He mustn't leave early.

Language Points Notice that we say in English:

She must type some letters *first*.
He must take some letters to the post-office *first*.

We can say too:
First she must type some letters.
First he must take some letters to the post-office.

Notice too, that we say:
Mr Dean is *away* on business.

We can say, too:
He's *out of town* on business.

Exercise 2,001 (two thousand and one)

Look at these sentences.

Mr Dean asked Miss Brown to pay the cleaning-woman.
What must Miss Brown do?
She must pay the cleaning-woman.

Mr Dean told John not to arrive late.
What mustn't John do?
He mustn't arrive late.

Respond to these sentences in the same way.

1. Mr Davis told his wife not to go to the cinema.
   What mustn't his wife do?
2. Miss Brown asked John to open the safe.
   What must John do?

72

3. Mrs Gray asked her friend to buy a kilo of coffee.
What must Mrs Gray's friend do?   (She . . .)

4. John's mother told him to get up at six o'clock.
What must John do?

5. Mr Johnson told his secretary not to answer the letter.
What mustn't his secretary do?

6. I asked you not to listen to the radio.
What mustn't you do?

7. The teacher told us to write our names in our books.
What must we do?

8. Mr Dean told his wife not to drink much wine.
What mustn't she do?

9. Mr Collins told his wife and her friend to wait for the bus.
What must they do?

10. Mr Johnson asked the office-boy to clean the filing cabinet.
What must the office-boy do?

Exercise 2,039   (two thousand and thirty-nine)

Listen to your teacher.

Reading Mr Dean arrived at the office early last Tuesday. He drank a cup of coffee quickly. Then he said to Miss Brown: 'I must travel to Brussels urgently today. I must dictate some letters immediately.'

Miss Brown knows shorthand very well. She took the letters correctly. Then Mr Dean left the office in a hurry at ten o'clock. Miss Brown typed the letters slowly afterwards.

Mr Van den Berg telephoned from Amsterdam at eleven o'clock. He said: 'I must talk to Mr Dean immediately.' Miss Brown answered: 'I'm sorry, Mr Dean left for Brussels at ten o'clock.'

Mr Van den Berg said: 'I must contact Mr Dean at once.'

Miss Brown looked at her diary and gave Mr Van den Berg the telephone number of the Brussels office. Mr Van den Berg rang off.

Miss Brown said to John afterwards: 'I don't like Mr Van den Berg very much. He spoke to me rudely.'

Language Points Look at this chart. In English we say *how, when* or *where* something happens at the end of the sentence. First we say *how*, then *where*, then *when*. But look at the sentence marked with † and with *.

*After verbs like 'go', 'travel', 'arrive', etc., the place comes first.
e.g.   I must travel to Brussels urgently today.

†Small units of time appear in front of large units of time.
e.g.   He arrived here at ten o'clock this morning.
       We telephoned from Santiago at four o'clock yesterday.

	HOW?	WHERE?	WHEN?
Mr Dean arrived*		at the office	†early last Tuesday.
He drank a cup of coffee	quickly.		
I must dictate some letters			immediately
Miss Brown knows shorthand	very well.		
She took the letters	correctly.		
Then he left the office	in a hurry		at ten o'clock.
Miss Brown typed the letters	slowly		afterwards.
Mr Van den Berg telephoned		from Amsterdam	at eleven o'clock.
I must talk to Mr Dean			immediately.
Mr Dean left		for Brussels	at ten o'clock.
I must contact Mr Dean			at once.
Miss Brown said to John			
'I don't like Mr Van den Berg	very much.		
He spoke to me	rudely.'		

Exercise 2,415   (two thousand, four hundred and fifteen)

Put the words in these sentences in the correct order.

1. at the grocer's   in packets   we buy coffee.
2. without sugar   this morning   she drank her tea.
3. this morning   at the grocer's   I was.
4. to the Odeon Cinema   last night   my wife and I went.
5. yesterday   at the florist's   we didn't buy any flowers.
6. before lunch   very quickly   at the office   Miss Brown typed some letters.
7. at the office   early   John arrived.
8. Last week   at the butcher's   on Friday   Jean paid for the meat.
9. In Brussels   yesterday   at nine o-clock   it rained.
10. every Friday   at the cafe   Jean meets Caroline.
11. last night   at John's house   he drank a bottle of wine.
12. quickly   this morning   we had breakfast.

Exercise 2,744   (two thousand, seven hundred and forty-four)

Answer your teacher's questions, using these words.

HOW	WHERE	WHEN
quickly	to/at the office	at — o'clock
well, very well	to/from London, Brussels, etc.	today
urgently	to/at the cinema	yesterday
in a hurry		in the morning
correctly		afternoon
very much		evening
rudely		immediately
		at once
		afterwards

Reading   What is Mr Johnson's programme tomorrow?

He's flying to Zurich. Mr Schulz is meeting him at the airport and they're having lunch together. Afterwards they're driving to Lucerne, where a conference is taking place. The firm's salesmen are meeting, and they're discussing the sales policy for next year. Mr Johnson's giving a talk. Mr Johnson and Mr Schulz are staying at the Grand Hotel in Lucerne. Mr Johnson's returning to London the next day because he's very busy. His secretary's not going to Switzerland with him. She's staying in London because she must type a lot of letters.

Exercise 4,279   (four thousand, two hundred and seventy-nine)

1. What's Mr Johnson doing tomorrow?
2. Who's meeting him in Zurich?
3. Are they driving to Lucerne immediately?
4. Why are Mr Johnson and Mr Schulz going to Lucerne?   **(Because)**
5. Why are the firm's salesmen meeting?
6. Is Mr Johnson doing anything at the Conference?
7. Where are Mr Johnson and Mr Schulz staying?
8. When's Mr Johnson returning to London?
9. Is Mr Johnson's secretary going to Switzerland?
10. Why's she staying in London?

Exercise 5,011   (five thousand and eleven)

Look at these examples.

Are you coming to class tomorrow?   (No)
No, I'm not.
Why not?   (there are no classes)
Because there are no classes tomorrow.

Are you going to the cinema tonight? (Yes)
Yes, I am.
Why? (I want to see the film)
Because I want to see the film.

Now respond to these sentences in the same way.

1. Are the salesmen discussing sales policy? (Yes)
    (Sales must grow next year)

2. Are you going to Paris next week? (No)
    (There's a sales conference in London)

3. Are you flying to Copenhagen tomorrow? (Yes)
    (My husband is going there)

4. Are you staying at the Ritz Hotel in Copenhagen? (No)
    (My husband doesn't like the Ritz)

5. Are you returning to London afterwards? (Yes)
    (I must meet my friend there on Thursday)

6. Did you go to Tossa de Mar last year? (Yes)
    (I go there every year)

7. Did Mr Johnson drive to Lucerne after lunch? (No)
    (He wanted to stay in Zurich)

8. Does Jean eat many chips? (No)
    (She doesn't want to get fat)

9. Does Miss Brown like Mr Van den Berg? (No)
    (He spoke to her rudely)

10. Could Miss Brown type the letters quickly? (Yes)
    (She knows shorthand very well)

Exercise 6,321   (six thousand three hundred and twenty-one)

Do you remember Richard in Lesson Seventeen. Look again at the pictures and the story about Richard on page 50.

Look at this example.

Richard stood up.
Why?
Because the teacher told him to.

Now answer these questions in the same way.

Richard went to the blackboard. Why?
Richard took the chalk. Why?
Richard wrote his name. Why?

Exercise 7,444   (seven thousand four hundred and forty-four)

Listen to your teacher.

Conversation   Mrs Jones is John's neighbour. She's a gossip. Mrs Taylor is Mrs Jones' friend. She doesn't talk much.

Mrs Jones: You know John Moore, *don't you*?

Mrs Taylor: Yes, I think so.

Mrs Jones: He works at Wickham Engineering, *doesn't he*?

Mrs Taylor: Yes, I think so.

Mrs Jones: He's the office-boy there, *isn't he*?

Mrs Taylor: Yes, I think so.

Mrs Jones: He hasn't got a very good job there, *has he*?

Mrs Taylor: No, I don't think so.

Mrs Jones: You can't earn much in that job, *can you*?

Mrs Taylor: No, I don't think so.

Mrs Jones: He comes home late every night, *doesn't he*?

Mrs Taylor: Does he?

Mrs Jones: He came home late last night, *didn't he*?

Mrs Taylor: Did he? I don't know.

Mrs Jones: I don't like the Moores very much, *do you*?

Mrs Taylor: Don't you? I like them.

Exercise 9,000   (nine thousand)

don't you?
doesn't he?
is there?
isn't he?
has he?
can you?   etc.

These are question-tags. Add question-tags to the following sentences.

1. Peter took the letters to the post-office.
2. Mr Dean's the manager.
3. There isn't anything else.
4. They have coffee together every week.
5. She doesn't mind.
6. He arrives at the office at half-past eight.
7. John hasn't got a car.
8. The two boys are listening to the radio.
9. She bought a dozen eggs.
10. Mrs Gray didn't buy a bottle of wine.
11. The grocer doesn't sell much coffee.
12. It's a good film.
13. That picture belongs to you.
14. Mr Davis and his wife didn't like the film.
15. He's having a swim.
16. It isn't raining.
17. You can speak Spanish.
18. The clerk couldn't understand David.
19. He told you to clean the typewriter.
20. Miss Brown must telephone Mr Johnson.
21. John mustn't arrive late.
22. Mr Dean left for Brussels at ten o'clock.
23. Miss Brown doesn't like Mr Van den Berg.
24. She knows shorthand very well.
25. Mr Van den Berg wanted to speak to Mr Dean urgently.

Exercise 9,001 (nine thousand and one)

Give answers to the sentences with question-tags in Exercise 9,000. Answer 'Yes, I think so' or 'No, I don't think so'.

Reading   Mr Johnson *is going to give* a talk at the sales-conference. He's *going to say* the following:

'This year we*'re going to launch* a new product on the market in Western Europe. It's *going to be* a very good product, a new antibiotic. We*'re going to call* it Marvomycin. The salesmen of the company *are going to sell* it everywhere on the Continent. We're selling it in Great Britain already, and it's *going to be* a success here, too. Chemists everywhere *are going to sell* a lot of it.'

Mr Johnson*'s going to talk* for half an hour, but we*'re not going to give* you the rest of the talk here, because you *aren't going to understand* it.

Exercise 11,427   (eleven thousand four hundred and twenty-seven)

Answer the following questions.

1. Who is going to give a talk at the sales conference?
2. What is the company going to launch on the market in Europe?
3. What is the name of the product going to be?
4. Where are the salesmen going to sell it?
5. Is it going to be a success on the Continent?
6. What are chemists going to do?
7. For how long is Mr Johnson going to talk?
8. Why isn't the writer of the passage going to give you the rest of the talk?

Exercise 36,162   (thirty-six thousand one hundred and sixty-two)

Listen to your teacher.

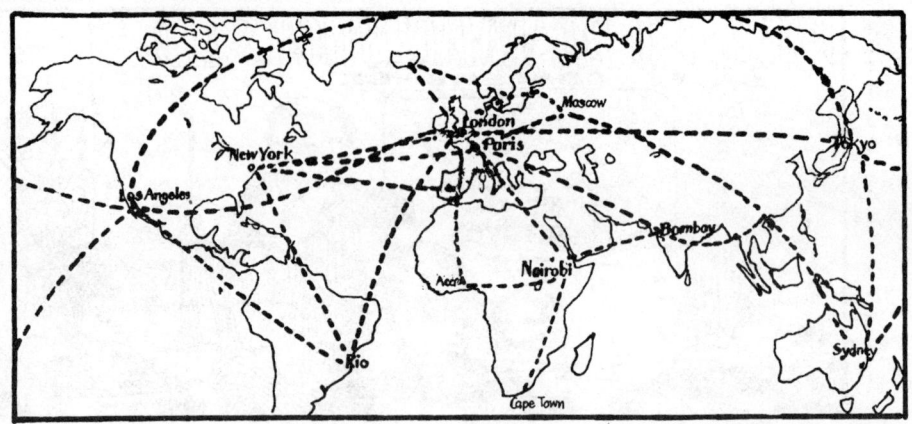

Read these sentences

Tokyo's a long way from London.
Is Tokyo far from London?
Yes, it's a long way.

Paris isn't far from London.
Is Paris far from London?
No, it's not far.

Listen to your teacher.

Reading   When Mr Dean returned from Brussels, he went to the office. When he walked in, Miss Brown *wasn't typing* letters. She *was reading* a newspaper. John *was sitting* at his desk and smoking a cigarette. Mrs Turner the cleaning-woman *wasn't working*. She *was sitting* on the edge of John's desk and *talking* to John. When Mr Dean walked in, nobody *was working*. Mr Dean didn't say anything, except, 'Good afternoon.'

They answered: 'Good afternoon' and then began to work.

The verbs in italics are in the past continuous tense.

Exercise 347,783
(three hundred and forty-seven thousand seven hundred and eighty-three)

Look at the reading and answer the following questions.

1.   What did Mr Dean do when he returned from Brussels?
2.   When he walked in, was Miss Brown typing letters?
3.   What was she doing?
4.   What was John doing?
5.   When Mr Dean walked in, was anybody working?
6.   What did Mr Dean say?
7.   What did Miss Brown, John and Mrs Turner say?
8.   What did they all do then?

Exercise 1,412,025
(one million, four hundred and twelve thousand and twenty-five)

Put the correct past continuous tense forms into the following sentences.

1.   While I (work), they (have) a good time.
2.   What (you do) while I was in Brussels?
3.   You (answer) the telephone when I arrived.

4. I met him when I (travel) to Paris.
5. Who (you talk) to when I saw you?
6. What (those people look) at when we drove past?
7. He (listen) to the radio when I left.
8. We (wait for) the bus when it began to rain.
9. While I (sign) the cheque, he (look) for the money.
10. Where (I sit) when you saw me in the cinema?

Exercise 8,357,168
(eight million, three hundred and fifty-seven thousand, one hundred and sixty-eight)

Listen to your teacher.

Conversation   Mr Johnson is arriving at a hotel.

Receptionist: Good evening, Sir.

Johnson: Good evening. My name is Johnson. My secretary telephoned yesterday and reserved a room for tonight.

Receptionist: One moment, Sir. Ah, yes. We reserved you Room No. 204. It's at the front and hasn't got a bathroom. But this morning we had a cancellation. Would you prefer to take Room 209 on the same floor? That is at the back and has got a bathroom.

Johnson: Yes, give me that room, please. I'd like a bathroom.

Receptionist: Certainly, Sir. Would you kindly complete this form, please?

Johnson: Would you lend me a pen?

Receptionist: Yes, Sir. Here you are.

Johnson: Thank you.

Receptionist: Would you like dinner, Sir?

Johnson: No, thank you. But I'd like a whisky and soda. Would you send it to my room?

Receptionist: With pleasure, Sir. Would you like ice with it?

Johnson: Yes, I would.

Receptionist: Very well, Sir. The porter is taking your suitcases to your room. Would you take the lift on the right?

Johnson: Thank you. Goodnight.

Receptionist: Goodnight, Sir.

Language Points Note the following points from the passage.

1. Room No. 204 is *at the front*
   Room No. 209 is *at the back*

2. The receptionist says: 'Good evening' to Mr Johnson when he arrives, and he answers: 'Good evening'. When he goes to his room, to sleep, they say 'Goodnight'.

3. In English we can say: lend me your pen.
   send a whisky to my room.
   But it is polite to say: Would you lend me your pen?
   Would you send a whisky to my room?

4. We sometimes place 'please' at the end of these sentences, or put in the word 'kindly': Would you lend me your pen, *please*?
   Would you *kindly* send a whisky to my room?

 Note carefully the position of 'kindly'.

Exercise A Now change these sentences into polite forms, inserting 'please' or 'kindly'.

1. Give me your address.
2. Write me a letter.
3. Pass the bread.
4. Take this letter to the post-office.
5. Carry my suitcase to the lift.

The polite answer to these polite requests is:

'Certainly' or 'Very well' or 'With pleasure'.

Repeat the polite forms in the above exercise, and give a polite answer.

Now do the following examples in the same way, giving the polite answers, too.

6. Lend me your suitcase.
7. Reserve a room at the Ritz Hotel for tomorrow.
8. Cancel that reservation.
9. Send that file to my office.
10. Put that coffee on my desk.

Exercise B (Revision) Note the following examples.

Type 1. Send a whisky and soda to Mr Johnson.
Type 2. Send him a whisky and soda.
Type 3. Send it to Mr Johnson.

Type 1.	Give the bread to John.
Type 2.	Give him the bread.
Type 3.	Give it to John.

Now change each of the following Type 1 sentences into Type 2 and Type 3 sentences.

1. Lend your pen to the receptionist.   (The receptionist is a girl)
2. She gives presents to her friend every week.   (The friend is a man)
3. Would you give this file to Mr Dean, please?
4. Buy those dresses for your daughters.
5. Would you kindly lend that typewriter to my secretary?
6. The hotel reserved these rooms for the visitors.
7. Take this letter to my sister.
8. The salesmen gave this watch to the manager.
9. My secretary must find that letter for the Sales Manager.
10. We must give this pen to Uncle Jim.
11. Mr Dean lent his umbrella to the office-boy.
12. She sent a telegram to Mr and Mrs Johnson.

Exercise C
(Revision)

Note the following examples.

| Type 4. | He gives presents to *his friend*. |
| Type 5. | I'm sorry. Who does he give them to? |

Now turn these Type 4 sentences into Type 5 sentences.

1. He is talking to *my sister*.
2. Mr Dean is looking for *his pen*.
3. He goes to *London* every week.
4. I am listening to *a good radio-programme*.
5. She's looking for *my brother's children*.
6. He is giving a file to *his secretary*.
7. He comes from *Manchester*.
8. I'm looking at *the blackboard*.
9. This coat belongs to *the teacher*.
10. The receptionist is sending a whisky to *Mr Johnson*.

Test for Lessons Twenty-one to Thirty

Exercise A   Look at these sentences.

Type Q.   Would you like a drink?   (Yes)
Type R.   Yes, please, I would.

Type Q.   Would you like a drink?   (No)
Type S.   No, thank you, not just now.

Type Q.   Do you like these flowers?   (Yes)
Type T.   Yes, I do. I like them very much.

Type Q.   Do you like these flowers?   (No)
Type U.   No. I'm afraid I don't like them at all.

Give Type R, S, T or U responses to the following Type Q sentences.

1.   Would you like some ice?   (Yes)
2.   Do you like soup?   (No)
3.   Would you like a glass of whisky?   (No)
4.   Would you like some bread?   (No)
5.   Do you like Sales Conferences?   (No)
6.   Would you like a cup of coffee?   (Yes)
7.   Do you like your neighbours?   (Yes)
8.   Do you like New York?   (Yes)

Exercise B   Look at these sentences.

Type V.   The chemist said to me, '*Please take* the antibiotic.'
Type W.   The chemist *asked* me to take the antibiotic.
Type X.   I must take the antibiotic.

Type V.   The Belgian said to our office-boy, '*Take* the letters to the post-office.'
Type W.   The Belgian *told* our office-boy to take the letters to the post-office.
Type X.   The office-boy must take the letters to the post-office.

Now give Type W and X sentences for these Type V sentences.

1.   Mr Dean said to Miss Brown, 'Please telephone our manager in Zurich.'
2.   I said to the waiter, 'Bring me a glass of whisky.'
3.   My neighbour said to the waiter, 'Please don't put any ice in the whisky.'
4.   The boss said to me, 'Call the salesmen to a sales conference.'
5.   I said to my secretary, 'Drive me to the airport.'
6.   The receptionist said to the cleaning woman, 'Please clean the counter.'
7.   He said to the clerk, 'Write that in the diary.'
8.   The receptionist said to me, 'Please don't fill in the form.'

Put the words in these sentences in the correct order.

1. to the Continent   immediately   I must travel.
2. yesterday   at the grocer's   we bought some coffee.
3. Last week   on Wednesday   rudely   he spoke to me.
4. in a hurry   to Brussels   yesterday   he flew.
5. without sugar   this afternoon   she drank her tea.
6. very quickly   today   at the hotel   I had lunch.

Exercise D   Look at these examples.

Are you going to New York tomorrow?   (Yes)
Yes, I am.
Why?   (There's a sales conference there)
Because there's a sales conference there.

Are you meeting him at Zurich?   (No)
No, I'm not.
Why not?   (He's travelling to Lucerne)
Because he's travelling to Lucerne.

Now ask and answer these questions in the same way, using the words in brackets.

1. Did he visit Spain in August?   (No) (He likes Switzerland)
2. Do you like my neighbour?   (No) (She's a gossip)
3. Are you staying at the Ritz tonight?   (Yes) (They haven't got any rooms at the Savoy)
4. Would you like your coffee without sugar?   (Yes) (I don't want to get fat)

Exercise E   Add question-tags to these sentences.

1. It's a long way to Manchester.
2. You take ice in your whisky.
3. We aren't launching that antibiotic this year.
4. You didn't understand that conversation.
5. You never listen to the radio.
6. This is my ticket.
7. You work at Wickham Engineering.
8. You signed that cheque.
9. You don't smoke much.
10. You didn't arrive at the hotel late last night.
11. He earns a lot.
12. The cleaning-woman drives a car.
13. You weren't looking at the map.

Exercise F   Read this passage.

When David arrived at the Sales Conference, the salesmen were discussing the new product. Mr Dean wasn't listening. He was dictating something into the dictaphone.

Now answer these questions.

1. What was happening when David arrived at the Sales Conference?
2. What wasn't Mr Dean doing?
3. What was he doing?

Exercise G Read this passage.

My friend is flying to New York tonight. He's going to stay at the Ritz. I'm going to telephone the manager there.

Now answer these questions.

1. What's your friend doing tonight?
2. What hotel's he going to stay at?
3. Who are you going to telephone to?

Exercise H Look at these sentences.

Type A. Lend your pen to me, please.
Type B. Would you kindly lend me your pen?

Now turn these Type A sentences into Type B sentences.

1. Give your dictaphone to me, please.
2. Write a letter to me from that hotel, please.
3. Send my secretary to Mr Dean, please.
4. Buy some files for me, please.
5. Reserve a room for our manager, please.

Vocabulary introduced in Lessons 21 to 30

(I'm) afraid	cancel	correctly	everywhere
airport	cancellation	the Continent	example
Amsterdam	cashier	dialogue	except
antibiotic	change (v)	diary	far
away	chemist	discuss	firm (n)
back (of building, etc.)	cheque	drive (v)	first
begin	clean (v)	early	floor (storey)
Belgian	cleaning-woman	earn	(the) following
Brussels	complete (v)	edge	form
call (v)	conference	Engineering	front
can	contact (v)	entertain	Good evening
	Copenhagen	Europe	Goodnight

gossip (person)
Great Britain
greengrocer
Here you are
how long?
(in a) hurry
ice
immediately
italics
job
kindly
late
launch (v)
lend
lift (n)
London
(a) long way
Lucerne
Manchester
map
market
moment
must
neighbour

New York
night
No, thank you
not just now
number
out of town
Paris
pay (v)
please
(with) pleasure
policy
polite
porter
poster
prefer
product
programme
question-tag
quickly
read
receptionist
request (n)
reserve (v)
reservation (n)

rest (remainder)
restaurant
return (v)
ring off
rudely
sales
Santiago
sir
sleep (v)
slowly
soda
(I'm) sorry
soup
speak
stand up
start
stay
steak
story
success
suitcase
Switzerland
take place
telegram

telephone (v)
tell
think
(I) think so
Tokyo
tomorrow
tonight
umbrella
understand
urgently
very well (obedient
    response)
view
visitor
walk
watch (n)
way
Western
whisky
world
writer

Dates   Revise the numbers up to a hundred.

In *Lesson Twenty* you learnt the names of the months in English. In the letter John wrote to his Uncle Jim in Lesson Nineteen, he wrote '14th August 1972'. But we say:

the fourteenth of August, nineteen seventy-two

We also write, for example:

December 4th, 1969

And we say:

December the fourth, nineteen sixty-nine

Exercise A   Now say these dates.

a)   11th January, 1948.
b)   July 7th, 1923.
c)   25th August, 1953.
d)   1st March, 1974.
e)   8th April, 1964.
f)   21st September, 1971.
g)   October 19th, 1984.
h)   June 12th, 1923.
i)   6th May, 1935.
j)   17th November, 1957.
k)   February 29th, 1960.
l)   25th December, 1970.

Reading

When Mr Johnson goes to Paris he takes the plane in the morning. He arrives in time for lunch and does his business there in the afternoon. He returns to London in the evening. He left for Paris on the morning of Monday, 2nd January. The weather was very cold. There was frost, snow and fog. The planes couldn't take off.

He took the train and the ship. The train from London to Dover was late. The sea at Dover was rough and the ship for Calais could not leave. At twelve o'clock at night Mr Johnson was still in Dover. The ship left on the afternoon of 3rd January at about three o'clock. The sea was still very rough.

When Mr Johnson arrived at Calais, it was dark. The train from Calais to Paris took a very long time, because the weather was still very bad. It arrived in Paris on Wednesday morning. It was a very bad journey and Mr Johnson was tired.

Language Points

Notice that we say:

in the morning
in the afternoon
in the evening
at night

but we say:

on the morning of Monday 2nd January
on the afternoon of 3rd January
on Wednesday morning
on the night of 5th December
on Sunday night

Exercise B Put *on*, *in*, *at* in the following sentences.

1. David didn't come to the office .... Wednesday morning.
2. He arrived in London .... night.
3. I don't work .... the morning.
4. The conference began .... the afternoon of 25th April.
5. He's taking the plane to Rome .... Sunday night.
6. The ship was still at Dover .... Tuesday morning.
7. Mr and Mrs Dean go to the cinema .... the evening.
8. Mr Van den Berg telephoned .... the afternoon.
9. You didn't come to class .... the afternoon of 21st March.
10. What did you do .... the evening?

Exercise C   Form sentences using these words.

1. Mrs Dean meets Mrs Gray.   morning/Friday
2. Mr Johnson flew to Brussels.   afternoon
3. The ship left.   afternoon/Tuesday, 6th January.
4. She doesn't work.   night
5. My holiday is going to begin.   12th August/evening

Exercise D   Listen to your teacher.

Reading

When Mr Dean was away on business, John had to clean the typewriter.

When Mr Dean returned, John had to do a great many other things. He had to do a great deal of work.

He had to go to the bank in order to cash a cheque for Mr Dean.

He had to go to the post-office in order to post some letters.

He had to spend money in order to do these things.

When he came back to the office, John had to make a list of these items, and Miss Brown had to have a look at the list in order to check the items.

Exercise A   Answer the following questions.

1. What did John have to do while Mr Dean was away?
2. How did he have to work when Mr Dean returned?
3. Where did he have to go in order to cash Mr Dean's cheque?
4. Where did he have to go in order to post the letters?
5. Why did he have to spend the money? (He had to spend money in order ....)
6. Why did he have to make a list of these items? (Because ...)
7. What did Miss Brown have to do in order to check the items?
8. Where do you go in order to buy meat?
9. What did you have to do at the beginning of this lesson?
10. Did you have to wait for the bus today?

Language Points   Look at these sentences.

He had to do *a great many* things.
He had to do *a great deal of* work.

We use *a great many* with plurals.
and *a great deal of* with singulars.
and *a great deal* when nothing follows in the singular.

Exercise B   Look at these examples.

I don't smoke much.
Oh yes, you do. You smoke a great deal.

We haven't got many products on the market.
Oh yes, we have. We've got a great many products on the market.

Respond to these sentences in the same way.

1.   It didn't snow much yesterday.
2.   We didn't discuss many things.
3.   He didn't sign many letters.
4.   He doesn't travel much.
5.   They aren't going to order much detergent.
6.   He doesn't ask many questions.
7.   We aren't going to stay in many hotels.
8.   She doesn't eat much.
9.   You didn't enclose many photographs.   (Oh, yes, I....)
10.   I didn't telephone many people.   (Oh, yes you ....)

Exercise C   Listen to your teacher.

Conversation   When Mr Dean was in Brussels, he telephoned his wife's friend, Mademoiselle Verhaeren. They spoke English, because Mademoiselle Verhaeren speaks English very well. Here is their conversation.

Mr Dean: Hallo. Is that Mademoiselle Verhaeren?

Mlle Verhaeren: Yes, it is. Who's speaking?

Mr Dean: Harold Dean. How are you?

Mlle Verhaeren: Very well, thank you. It's nice to hear you. How are you, and how's Eleanor?

Mr Dean: We're very well, too.

Mlle Verhaeren: That's good. Are you coming to see me?

Mr Dean: No, I'm afraid not. I'm in Brussels on a very short visit.

Mlle Verhaeren: That's a pity.

Mr Dean: On my next visit to Brussels, my wife is coming with me.

Mlle Verhaeren: Please bring her to see me. Come and have dinner with me in my flat next time.

Mr Dean: Thank you very much, we should like to. We like your cooking very much. Mademoiselle, please excuse me. I must go. The plane is taking off for London in ten minutes.

Mlle Verhaeren: Very well. Thank you for the telephone-call. I'm looking forward to your next visit.

Mr Dean: Thank you. My wife and I are, too.

Mlle Verhaeren: Please give my best wishes to Eleanor. Goodbye.

Mr Dean: Thank you. Goodbye.

Conversation   When Mr Dean returned to London, his wife asked him:

Mrs Dean: Did you telephone Mademoiselle Verhaeren?

Mr Dean: Yes, I did.

Mrs Dean: How was she?

Mr Dean: She said she was very well. I told her we were very well, too.

Mrs Dean: Didn't you go to see her?

Mr Dean: No, I told her I didn't have time. I said I was on a very short visit.

Mrs Dean: What did she say?

Mr Dean: She said it was a pity. I told her you were coming with me next time.

Mrs Dean: What did she say?

Mr Dean: She asked me to take you to see her. She invited us to have dinner with her.

Mrs Dean: What else did she say?

Mr Dean: Nothing. I told her the plane was taking off in ten minutes. I told her I must go.

Mrs Dean: What did she say?

Mr Dean: She said she was looking forward to our next visit, and she asked me to give you her best wishes.

Mrs Dean: I must write to her.

Exercise A   Look at the conversation between Mr Dean and Mademoiselle Verhaeren. Answer these questions. Do not look at the conversation between Mr and Mrs Dean.

1. What did Mlle Verhaeren say when Mr Dean asked her how she was?
2. When she asked how Mr and Mrs Dean were, what did Mr Dean say?
3. Was Mr Dean going to see Mademoiselle Verhaeren?
4. He told her why. What did he say?
5. What did Mlle Verhaeren say when Mr Dean said he couldn't go and see her?
6. What did he tell her about his next visit to Brussels?
7. What did Mlle Verhaeren invite him and Mrs Dean to do on their next visit?
8. What did Mr Dean tell Mlle Verhaeren about her cooking?
9. Why did Mr Dean tell Mlle Verhaeren he had to go? What did he say?
10. What did Mlle Verhaeren say about Mr and Mrs Dean's next visit?
11. What did she ask Mr Dean to give to Mrs Dean?

Notice this sentence: I told her I *must* go.
In this kind of sentence 'must' does not change.

Exercise B   Look at these sentences.

Type A.   My wife's coming with me next time.   (I   her)
Type B.   *I told her* you were coming with me next time.
Type C.   *I said* you were coming with me next time.

Turn the following sentences into Type B and Type C sentences, using the words given and making other necessary changes.

1. I'm coming to your house for dinner.   (Mr Dean   Mr Johnson)
2. The sales conference is taking place at Lucerne.   (The sales manager   his secretary)
3. I can type it immediately.   (Miss Brown   Mr Dean)
4. David is spending his holiday at Tossa de Mar.   (Mrs Jones   Mrs Taylor)
5. I change my cheques at that bank.   (He   me)
6. Mr Dean's not going to Paris.   (The office-boy   the secretary)
7. The plane takes off at four o'clock.   (The receptionist   Mr Johnson)
8. We must buy some flowers.   (Mrs Gray   Mrs Dean)
9. I can't pay you.   (The clerk   David)
10. I'm very well.   (Mlle Verhaeren   Mr Dean)

Exercise C   Listen to your teacher.

Reading　Do you remember that in Lesson 28, Mr Johnson announced the launching of Marvomycin?

Marvomycin is the firm's *newest* product. The firm has got an *older* antibiotic on the market too. It's called Penilongin, and at present it sells in *larger* quantities than Marvomycin. Marvomycin is *better* because doctors can use it in a *larger* number of cases. It is the *best* antibiotic on the market for some illnesses. Washford Pharmaceuticals is *smaller* than *more famous* firms like Parke Davis or Ciba, but Mr Johnson thinks that Marvomycin is going to make Washford *bigger* and *richer*.

Language Points　Look at the words in italics in this passage.

Now look at these sentences.

Marvomycin is a *new* product.
It's *newer* than Penilongin.
It's Washford's *newest* product.

John has a *good* salary.
Miss Brown earns a *better* salary.
Mr Dean earns the *best* salary.

Do you remember the Davis family in Lesson Ten?
Look back at Lesson 10, page 23.

Alan's the baby. He's the *youngest* child.
Jill's seven years old. She's *older* than Alan.
Donald's ten. He's the *oldest*.

Alan's the *smallest* child.
Jill's *bigger*.
Donald's the *biggest*.

You already know the following adjectives. Now learn their comparative and superlative forms:

POSITIVE	COMPARATIVE	SUPERLATIVE
small	smaller	smallest
fat	fatter	fattest
good	better	best
bad	worse	worst
nice	nicer	nicest
hot	hotter	hottest
warm	warmer	warmest
cold	colder	coldest
tall	taller	tallest
short	shorter	shortest
thin	thinner	thinnest
fair	fairer	fairest
good-looking	better-looking	best-looking
ugly	uglier	ugliest
long	longer	longest
new	newer	newest
old	older	oldest
large	larger	largest
big	bigger	biggest
rich	richer	richest
young	younger	youngest
old	elder/older	eldest/oldest
kind	kinder	kindest

There are also adjectives of another type.

different	more different	most different
necessary	more necessary	most necessary
correct	more correct	most correct
tired	more tired	most tired
famous	more famous	most famous

Look at these sentences.

A Jaguar is an expensive car.
A Mercedes Benz is more expensive than a Jaguar.
A Rolls Royce is the most expensive.

Exercise A   Now put the correct form of the adjective into the following sentences, and supply *than* where necessary.

1.   Mrs Gray is (fat) Mrs Dean.
2.   Alan is (small) child in the Davis family.
3.   Jean is (good-looking) Bill.

4. (short) way from London to Paris is through Dover.
5. Mrs Gray makes (good) cakes Mrs Dean.
6. Marvomycin is (new) Penilongin.
7. Parke-Davis is a (large) firm Washford Pharmaceuticals.
8. A Jaguar is (expensive) a Volkswagen, but a Rolls Royce is (expensive).
9. In January it is (warm) in Rome in London, but the weather is (hot) in Rio de Janeiro.
10. Donald is (tall) of the Davis children.
11. Mr Johnson had (bad) journey to Paris in January/in April.
12. Miss Brown's typing is (correct) mine.
13. Mrs Dean is (young) husband.
14. Mr Davis is (tall) Donald and Jill. Jill is (short) of all.
15. Mr Dean is nice, but Mrs Dean is (nice).
16. Donald is (old) child in the Davis family. Jill is his (young) sister.

Look at these pictures.
Look at your mask for the colours.

Mrs Dean's got a car.

←**Blue car**

Mrs Dean's car's small.
It's *a small one*.
It's blue.
It's *a blue one*.

Mr Dean's got a *bigger* one.

←**Black car**

Mr Dean's car's big.
It's *a big one*.
It's black.
It's *a black one*.

Mr Johnson's got *the biggest one*.

←**Grey car**

Mr Johnson's car's very big.
It's *a very big one*.
It's grey.
It's *a grey one*.

Look at this dialogue

One day Mr and Mrs Dean and Mr Johnson went to a party. They parked outside the house. Two small boys saw the three cars. Here is their conversation.

Tom: Look at those cars. I *like that black one.*
Bill: Look at *the big grey one.* That's *the best one.*
Tom: But *the blue one's* very nice.
Bill: Which is *the best one?*
Tom: The grey car's *the best one.* I like small cars, but I like *big ones* more.

Exercise B Look at these pictures. Answer the questions.

1. Which car do you like best?
2. Do you like small cars? (I like ....)
3. What colour do you like? (I like ....)

Now look at these pictures. Answer the questions.

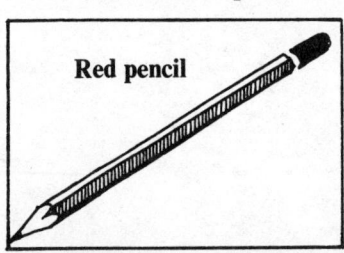
Red pencil

Blue pencil

4. Which pencil do you see on the left?
5. Which pencil do you see on the right?
6. Is the red pencil the shorter one?
7. Is the blue pencil the longer one?

Jean   Bill

8. Which picture shows Jean?   (The one on . . . .)
9. Which picture shows Bill?
10. Is Jean the short one?
11. Is Bill the fair one?
12. Do you like short men?
13. Do you like fair women?

Exercise C Now listen to your teacher.

Reading   Before he left Brussels by plane, Mr Dean *had sent* his wife a telegram in order to tell her the flight-number and the time of his arrival at London Airport. When the plane took off from Brussels, Mrs Dean *had* already *taken* her husband's car out of the garage, and was driving to the airport. She *had telephoned* the airline first. They told her the weather was good and the plane was leaving on time. When Mrs Dean arrived at the airport, the plane *had already landed*. It *had arrived* early. Mr Dean *had left* the plane, but he *hadn't passed* through the Customs. Mrs Dean had to wait till he *had cleared* Customs. After Mr Dean *had kissed* his wife, they got into the car and drove home.

Language Points   In the above passage, the verbs *in italics* are in the past perfect tense. When we are talking about the past, we use this tense to make it clear what happened first.

Example:

When Mrs Dean arrived at the airport, the plane *had* already *landed*.
(The plane landed first, then Mrs Dean arrived.)

After they *had kissed*, they got into the car and drove home.
(They kissed first, then got into the car.)

Exercise A   Answer these questions about the passage.

1. What had Mr Dean done before he left Brussels?
2. What had Mrs Dean done when the plane took off?
3. What had she done before she took the car out of the garage?
4. What had already happened when Mrs Dean arrived at the airport?
5. Had Mr Dean left the plane?
6. Had he passed through the customs?
7. Why did Mrs Dean have to wait?
8. What had they done when they got into the car?

Exercise B   Look at these sentences.

Type X.   First John had a bath, then he went out.   (After)
Type Y.   After John had had a bath, he went out.

Type X.   First he cleared Customs, then he drove away.   (before)
Type Y.   He had cleared Customs before he drove away.

Now turn the following Type X sentences into Type Y sentences using the Past Perfect tense for the first action.

1. First she telephoned, then she checked the list.   (before)
2. First Miss Brown paid the cleaning woman, then she closed the safe.   (As soon as)
3. First Mr Johnson sent a telegram, then he bought a newspaper. (When)
4. First the train left, then I arrived at the railway station.   (before)
5. First the firm launched the new antibiotic, then it began to get richer. (As soon as)
6. First the secretary typed the letters, then she went home.   (After)
7. First Tommy stood up, then the teacher came in.   (before)
8. First I had to go, then he finished.   (before)
9. First he finished, then we left the office.   (As soon as)
10. First Mr Johnson gave his talk, then they had dinner.   (When)

Exercise C   Write these numbers in words.

1. 143	3. 301,224	5. 19,146	7. 1st	9. 103rd
2. 2,245th	4. 70,703	6. 224,671	8. 22nd	10. 2,443,708

Reading

Miss Brown is never late for work. This is perhaps surprising, because she doesn't always go to work by the same route. Her father is a schoolteacher. When he goes to school, he sometimes takes his daughter to the railway-station by car and then she always continues the journey by train. She sometimes takes the bus. The bus passes her house and takes her straight to the office, but she doesn't often go by bus because it is slow, and she has to get out of bed early in order to catch it. Miss Brown usually goes by bus when her father is on holiday. Her brother frequently telephones and says he can take her by car. Her brother is a doctor, and he can often leave her at the office on his way to hospital. But the journey by road usually takes longer than the journey by train. Miss Brown nearly always returns home by train.

Language Points

Look at these sentences from the reading passage.

Miss Brown is *never* late for work.
This is *perhaps* surprising.
He *sometimes* takes his daughter to the railway-station by car.
She *always* continues the journey by train.
She *sometimes* takes the bus.
She doesn't *often* go by bus.
Her brother *frequently* telephones.
He can *often* leave her at the office.
The journey by car *usually* takes longer.
Miss Brown *nearly always* returns home by train.

The adverbs in italics are *mid-position adverbs*. Notice carefully their position in relation to the verbs.

Put these mid-position adverbs in their correct place in these sentences.

1. She comes here on Tuesday. (always)
2. He's on time for work. (always)
3. She goes to work by train. (frequently)
4. He's asleep. (perhaps)
5. She has dinner with me. (never)
6. He stays at that hotel. (rarely)
7. Mr Dean doesn't type letters. (usually)
8. It's better by rail. (usually)
9. He passes the house (often) but he stops (rarely).
10. He doesn't speak to me. (always)
11. Mr Johnson has a glass of beer. (never)
12. He eats at that restaurant. (often)

**Useful
Expressions** Look at these sentences from the reading passage. Notice the expressions in *italics*.

Miss Brown is never late *for work*.
She doesn't always go *to work* by the same route.
When he goes *to school* he sometimes takes his daughter to the railway-station *by car*, and then she always continues the journey *by train*.
She doesn't often go *by bus*.
He can take her *by car*.
He can often leave her at the office on his way to hospital, but the journey *by road* always takes a long time.
Miss Brown nearly always returns home *by rail*.

Look at these expressions, too.
He takes his daughter *to the railway-station* by car.
The bus takes her straight *to the office*.
He can often leave her *at the office*.

Notice that in English we say:
by car, by bus, by road, by rail, by air, by plane, by sea.

We also say:
in ink, in pencil, in shorthand, in longhand, on paper, on foot.

But we say:
at *the* office, to *the* office, to *the* railway-station, and also
to *the* theatre, to *the* cinema, to *the* airport (see Lesson 35)
to *the* bus-station, and so on.

We usually say:
to work, to school, to bed, to hospital.

and also, for example:
at work, in bed, out of hospital.

We also say:
'home' (meaning 'to our house') and 'at home' (meaning 'in our house').

Exercise B   Insert the correct expression in these sentences.

1. He arrived .... office late.
2. She went .... bed early.
3. When he was travelling to London .... car last week, he had an accident and had to go .... hospital.
4. Mr Dean always travels .... work .... train.
5. He is going to Stockholm .... plane tomorrow, but is travelling .... airport .... car.
6. Miss Brown never writes .... longhand .... office. She always writes .... shorthand.
7. We must go .... railway-station and travel .... rail. When we go .... theatre .... road, we can never find a parking-place.
8. Kindly confirm your cancellation .... paper.
9. When we travel .... road, we go .... bus-station .... car. When we travel .... rail we go .... railway-station .... foot.
10. You can't write that letter .... pencil.

Exercise C   Look at these sentences.

Miss Brown is *never* late for work.
Is Miss Brown *ever* late for work?
She *always* goes to work by the same route.
Does she *always* go to work by the same route?

Notice carefully the position of the words in *italics*. These are adverbs.

Now change these statements into questions, putting the adverbs in the correct position.

1. He takes his daughter by car.   (ever)
2. She continues the journey by train.   (usually)
3. She takes the bus.   (often)
4. Her brother telephones.   (ever)
5. He leaves her at the office.   (sometimes)
6. That man is the manager.   (perhaps)
7. She has to get out of bed early.   (often)
8. He had a bath.   (often)
9. Washford put new products on the market.   (frequently)
10. Mrs Dean meets him at the airport.   (always)

Exercise D   Put the whole reading passage on page 107 into the past simple
(Revision)   tense. Say what *happened*.

Conversation   Mr Dean is planning a business-trip to the United States. He's having a talk with Miss Brown, his secretary.

Mr Dean: Ah, Jean, sit down please. Next month I'll probably go to New York. Mr Grant knows. He'll be in charge during my absence.

Miss Brown: Yes, Mr Dean. Shall I book a flight for you?

Mr Dean: No, thank you, Jean. That won't be possible till next week. I don't know the day of my departure. We'll get a letter from Mr Bloom, our customer there, next week.

Miss Brown: Will Mrs Dean go with you?

Mr Dean: No, she won't. She'll spend the time with her friend in Brussels.

Miss Brown: Shall I make any arrangements?

Mr Dean: No, thank you, Jean. I'm telling you now because you'll handle the correspondence. I told Mr Grant this morning, but I shan't tell the other members of the staff.

Miss Brown: Very well. I shan't say anything to anybody.

Mr Dean: That's fine Jean. I'm not sure yet that I'm going.

Language Points   Notice the use of the verbs in the conversation. The short forms of the verbs appear in the conversation. Here are the long forms.

I'll probably *go* to New York.	*I shall* probably *go* to New York.
He'll be in charge during my absence.	*He will be* in charge during my absence.
That *won't be* possible.	That *will not be* possible.
We'll get a letter from Mr Bloom.	*We shall get* a letter from Mr Bloom.

She'll spend the time with her friend in Brussels. *She will spend* the time with her friend in Brussels.
You'll handle the correspondence. *You will handle* the correspondence.
I *shan't tell* the other members of the staff. I *shall not tell* the other members of the staff.
I *shan't say* anything to anybody. I *shall not say* anything to anybody.

Look at this table and learn it.

Affirmative		*Negative*		*Interrogative*
Long Form	*Short Form*	*Long Form*	*Short Form*	
I shall	I'll	I shall not	I shan't	Shall I?
We shall	We'll	We shall not	We shan't	Shall we?
You will	You'll	You will not	You won't	Will you?
He will	He'll	He will not	He won't	Will he?
She will	She'll	She will not	She won't	Will she?
It will	It'll	It will not	It won't	Will it?

Exercise A   Look at these sentences.

Type J.   Miss Brown is here   (tomorrow).
Type K.   Miss Brown will be here tomorrow.
Type L.   Miss Brown will not be here tomorrow.
Type M.   Will Miss Brown be here tomorrow?

Now turn these Type J sentences into Type K, L and M sentences.

1. Mr Dean is telling Mr Grant   (next week).
2. Mrs Dean is spending her holiday in Brussels   (in July).
3. He gets a letter from Mr Bloom   (next month).
4. Mr Bloom is our agent in New York   (next year).
5. It's possible   (next Thursday).
6. We know the day of our departure   (tomorrow).
7. You're making the arrangements   (immediately).
8. He's talking to the other members of staff   (this afternoon).
9. The assistant manager is in charge   (during his absence).
10. We're booking the flight   (at six o'clock).

Exercise B   Look at these sentences.

Type J.   Miss Brown's here.
Type N.   Miss Brown's here, isn't she?
Type O.   Miss Brown will be here, won't she?
Type P.   Miss Brown won't be here, will she?

111

Now turn the Type J sentences in EXERCISE A into Type N, O and P sentences.

Notice these special forms of the future tense.

Mr Dean *must go* to New York.
Mr Dean *will have to go* to New York.
Miss Brown *can type* those letters very quickly.
Miss Brown *will be able to* type those letters very quickly.

Exercise C   Put the following sentences into the future tense, using short forms.

1. I must talk to you immediately.
2. He can fly there.
3. We must make the arrangements quickly.

Use the long form for these sentences.

4. They can wait until his departure.
5. She must spend her holiday in London.
6. The bank can change that cheque.

Now put the above sentences into the negative and interrogative forms, using short forms for 1, 2, and 3, and long forms for 4, 5, and 6.

Exercise D   Look at these sentences.

Type R.   Mr Dean'll probably go to New York next month.   (Yes)
Type S.   Yes, he will.

Type R.   Mr Dean won't see Mr Bloom there.   (No)
Type S.   No, he won't.

Now turn these sentences into Type S and T sentences.

1. Miss Brown won't book a flight today.   (No)
2. Mr Dean'll get a letter from Mr Bloom next week.   (Yes)
3. Mrs Dean won't go to New York with her husband.   (No)
4. She'll go to Brussels.   (Yes)
5. She won't spend the time at an hotel.   (No)
6. She'll spend the time with her friend.   (Yes)
7. Miss Brown won't make any arrangements today.   (No)
8. Miss Brown'll handle the correspondence.   (Yes)
9. She won't tell the other members of the staff.   (No)
10. She won't say anything to anybody.   (No)

Exercise E   Listen to your teacher.

Conversation Read the conversation at the beginning of the last lesson again.

Language Points Now look at these sentences.

1. *If Mr Dean goes to New York*, Mr Grant will be in charge.
2. *If Mr Dean goes to New York*, Miss Brown will have to book a flight.
3. *If Mr Dean goes to New York*, his wife will spend the time in Brussels.
4. *If Mr Dean goes to New York*, he'll tell the other members of the staff.
5. *If Mr Dean doesn't go to New York*, his wife will stay at home.
6. *If Mr Dean doesn't go to New York*, his secretary won't have to make any arrangements.
7. *If Mr Dean doesn't get a letter from the customer*, he won't be able to give his secretary his instructions.

Notice that the first part of the sentence written in *italics* is in the present tense. Now compare the above sentences with the sentences below.

1. Mr Grant will be in charge if Mr Dean goes to New York.
2. Miss Brown will have to book a flight if Mr Dean goes to New York.
3. Mrs Dean will go to Brussels if her husband goes to New York.
4. Mr Dean will tell the other members of the staff if he goes to New York.
5. Mrs Dean will stay at home if her husband doesn't go to New York.
6. Miss Brown won't have to make any arrangements if her boss doesn't go to New York.
7. Mr Dean won't be able to give his secretary his instructions if he doesn't get a letter from Mr Bloom.

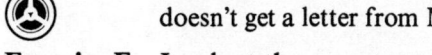

Exercise F Look at these sentences.

Type U. You telephone. He comes.
Type V. If you telephone, he will come.
Type W. He'll come if you telephone.

Now turn the following Type U sentences into Type V and W sentences. Use long forms of the verb on Type V sentences and short forms on Type W sentences.

1. John cleans the typewriter. Miss Brown types better.
2. It rains. We cannot go.
3. You post the letter today. He knows tomorrow.
4. We check the items. The list is correct.
5. Mr Johnson works hard. His talk is better.
6. Washford sell a lot of Marvomycin. The firm gets richer.
7. Mr Dean buys a Jaguar. He must sell his other car.
8. Miss Brown's brother drives her to the office. She arrives late.

9. You take the train to Paris. You do not see Monsieur Dupré.
10. They eat at that restaurant. They pay a great deal.
11. Your secretary books the plane. You can make a cancellation later.
12. You invite him to dinner. You increase sales of the new antibiotic.
13. Caroline eats a great many cakes. She gets fat.
14. You get fatter. You can never wear that pair of trousers.
15. You go to the bank. The manager sees you.
16. David is on holiday in July. He is not here for the Sales Conference.
17. He does not learn English. We cannot send him to London.
18. The train arrives at midday. We arrive after the beginning of his talk.
19. She does not tell me tomorrow. I never know.
20. He does not like the blue ones. We buy him some green ones.

Letter-writing   Read this letter.

H. BLOOM & SONS, INC.
417 East 11th Street
NEW YORK

14th July, 1972

Mr. H.F. Dean,   Your ref: HFD/JB/600
Manager,   Our ref: HB/C/WE/424
Wickham Engineering Co. Ltd.,
27 Wheat Street,
3rd Floor,
LONDON EC3H 5XB

Dear Mr. Dean,

Thank you for your letter of 9th July, 1972.

Here is the program for the first part of your visit. When you arrive at Kennedy Airport I shall meet you and take you to your hotel by car. We are reserving a room for you at the Manhattan Towers Hotel.

After you check in there, I shall wait for you in the hotel lounge. While you are having a bath and changing your clothes, Mr. Conrad S. Wright, our Purchasing Manager will come to the hotel. Then, as soon as you are ready, we shall be able to have a discussion about this company's next order from your firm.

I shall leave the rest of your program till you get there. We can talk about that while we are driving from the airport to the hotel.

We are looking forward to your visit.

Sincerely yours,

H. Bloom

H. Bloom
Managing Director

Notice two differences in British and American practice.

AMERICAN	BRITISH
Program	Programme
Sincerely yours	Yours sincerely (at the end of letters)

Now look at these sentences from the passage:

CLAUSE A	CLAUSE B
When you arrive at Kennedy Airport	I shall meet you.
After you check in there	I shall wait for you in the hotel lounge.
While you are having a bath and changing your clothes	Mr Wright will come to the hotel.
As soon as you are ready	We shall be able to have a discussion.

Notice that in each case, CLAUSE A begins with an expression like *when, as soon as, after, while, till* (temporal conjunctions), and the verb is in the Present Continuous or Present Simple Tense. CLAUSE B is in the Future Tense.

Notice, too, the following two sentences.

As soon as you are ready, we *shall be able to have* a discussion.
We *can talk* about that while we are driving from the airport to the hotel.

'Can' and 'must' sometimes have future meaning.

Compare the construction of these sentences with the IF-type sentences at the beginning of this lesson.

Exercise G Look at these examples.

Type X. What will happen when Mr Dean arrives at Kennedy Airport?
Type Y. Mr Bloom will meet him and take him to his hotel.

Now give Type Y answers to these Type X questions about the letter.

1. What will happen when Mr Dean checks in?
2. What will happen while Mr Dean is having a bath and changing his clothes?
3. What will happen as soon as Mr Dean is ready?
4. What will Mr Bloom leave till Mr Dean gets to New York?
5. What will Mr Bloom and Mr Dean talk about while they are driving from the airport to the hotel?

Exercise H Look at these examples.

> *Type Q.* When will Mr Bloom meet Mr Dean?
> *Type Z.* When he arrives at Kennedy Airport.

Now give Type Z answers to these Type Q questions about the letter.

1. When will Mr Bloom drive Mr Dean to his hotel?
2. When will Mr Bloom wait in the hotel lounge?
3. When will Mr Wright come to the Manhattan Towers Hotel?
4. When will Mr Dean, Mr Bloom and Mr Wright be able to have a discussion?
5. When will Mr Bloom and Mr Dean talk about the rest of Mr Dean's programme?

Exercise I Imagine that you are Mr Dean, and that Mr Bloom is coming to London for a discussion about his firm's next order. You will meet him at Heathrow Airport. He will stay at the London Hilton Hotel. After he checks in, you will wait for him. Mr Kelly, your firm's Chief Sales Manager, will come to the hotel for the discussion. You will talk about the rest of his programme while you are driving from Heathrow Airport to his hotel. Use the letter in this lesson as a model and write one to Mr Bloom about his visit.

Exercise J Listen to your teacher.

Conversation   One day, Mr Dean called Mr Grant to his office.

Mr Dean: Sit down please, Jack. You know that at the end of this year the lease of these offices will come to an end?

Mr Grant: Yes, Mr Dean. I know that.

Mr Dean: We shan't be able to renew the contract. In my opinion it would be a good idea if we moved out of London.

Mr Grant: If we moved to the country, it would reduce our costs.

Mr Dean: Exactly. We should pay less rent. We should be able to pay less in salaries. Of course some of the staff would leave the firm. They wouldn't want to move out of London.

Mr Grant: If we made a decision soon, we should be able to find other jobs for those people.

Mr Dean: Yes. At present this is only an idea, Jack. I should be grateful if you would think about it.

Language Points   Look at these sentences from the passage.

If the firm moved out of London	it would be a good idea. it would reduce the costs. they would pay less rent. they would be able to pay lower salaries. some of the staff would leave.
I should be grateful	if you would think about it.

Notice that the conversation is about a plan for the future. Mr Dean and Mr Grant are talking about an idea. They do not know if they are going to move out of London or not. They use 'should' or 'would' in their conversation.

But when Mr Dean talks about definite happenings in the future, he says:

The lease of these offices *will* come to an end. We *shan't* be able to renew the contract.

In Lesson 37 there were sentences such as:

If Mr Dean goes to New York, Mr Grant will be in charge.
Mr Dean won't be able to give his secretary her instructions if he doesn't get a letter from the agent.

Study this table of verbs.

Full Form	Short Form
I should go	I'd go
You would go	You'd go
He would go	He'd go
She would go	She'd go
It would go	It'd go
We would go	We'd go
They would go	They'd go

In the following exercises use long or short forms of the verb as you wish.

Exercise A   Look at these sentences.

What would happen if the firm moved out of London?
Type A.   If the firm moved out of London, it would reduce costs.
Type B.   Would it really reduce them?
Type C.   Yes, it would.

Now turn these sentences into Type A, B and C sentences. In the Type B sentences use pronoun objects where possible.

1.   What would happen if the lease of this office came to an end?
     (We – can – renew it)

2.   What would happen if Mr Dean bought a new car?
     (He – must – sell the old one)

3.   What would happen if the firm moved to the country?
     (We – can – pay lower salaries)

4.   What would happen if the firm moved out of London?
     (Some of the staff – leave – the – firm)

5.   What would happen if Mr Grant and Mr Dean made a decision soon?
     (They – can – find – jobs for those people)

Exercise B   Look at these examples.

Mr Grant's secretary isn't rich. She can't buy an expensive house.
Type E.   If Mr Grant's secretary were rich, she'd buy an expensive house.
Type F.   Of course she would.

Mr Dean likes that hotel. He always takes a room there.
Type E.   If Mr Dean didn't like that hotel, he wouldn't always take a room there.
Type F.   Of course he wouldn't.

Now turn these sentences into Type E and Type F sentences.

1. The firm sells Penilongin. We can pay our salesmen well.
2. It's quicker by rail. He always travels to Birmingham by train.
3. Mr Johnson isn't Brazilian. He doesn't drink much coffee.
4. David has got a lot of money at present. He will spend his holiday in Paris.
5. Mr Dean is in Amsterdam. We shall get a telephone-call from him.
6. We haven't got a cancellation. He can't have Room No. 407.
7. Rio de Janeiro is a nice city. They want to live there.
8. He's not here. We can't have a discussion.
9. He's ill. He must go to hospital.
10. The plane isn't late. The airline won't telephone me.
11. Miss Verhaeren is inviting us. We're going to her flat for dinner.
12. Mr Bloom isn't writing to Mr Dean. He won't go to New York.
13. We're not launching Marvomycin now. We shan't make much money.
14. Mr Dean drinks beer. He's getting fat.
15. There isn't a good film. We can't go to the cinema.

Exercise C   Look at these sentences.

Miss Brown is the manager's secretary. She can type well.
Type G.   Miss Brown wouldn't be the manager's secretary if she couldn't type well.
Type H.   She certainly wouldn't.

Now turn these into Type G and Type H sentences.

1. You understand me. I speak English.
2. David is going to the bank. There is some money in his account.
3. I shan't drink that coffee. It isn't hot.
4. Mrs Dean isn't going to the station. She doesn't know the time of Mr Dean's train.
5. The firm is moving out of London. It will reduce our costs.
6. John isn't buying a Jaguar. He hasn't got much money.

Exercise D   Listen to your teacher.

119

Reading One morning Mr Grant's secretary Vera, received a circular. It read like this:

BEAUTICARE COSMETICS LTD.,

62 Talbot Road,
Northampton, NN1 XP4

June 1973

Dear Madam,

We have pleasure <u>in enclosing</u> a sample of our fabulous new product <u>for removing</u> ugly hair from the body. We are sure that, <u>on applying</u> it, you will

Vera did not read any more. She said to Jean Brown: 'These firms insist *on sending* free samples, and I'm tired *of receiving* them.' Then she threw the circular and the sample into the wastepaper-basket.

Jean smiled and said: 'Oh, I don't object *to getting* them. If the firms marketed their products *without sending* free samples, they would have difficulty *in launching* them.'

Look at the words in *italics*. Then turn back to page 49 in Lesson Seventeen, Exercise 158. You will find these sentences.

What did Mr Dean do *before drinking* the beer?
What did he do *before paying* for the beer?
Where did he go *after drinking* the beer.

The first word of each pair *in italics* is a preposition. The second is a gerund. You must always use the gerund form when a verb immediately follows a preposition.

Exercise A Look at this example.

Type A. Thank you for (you took) that letter to the post-office.
Type B. Thank you for *taking* that letter to the post-office.

Now make these Type A sentences into Type B sentences.

1. We have pleasure in (we are informing) you that we are launching a new product.
2. On (he received) my telephone-call he placed the order.
3. He insisted on (he bought) me a cup of coffee.
4. I'm tired of (I'm always meeting) people at the airport.
5. She objected to (she received) free samples.
6. You can't market a new product without (you must send) samples.
7. In England you must pay for your beer before (you drink) it.
8. We shall have no difficulty in (we shall sell) Marvomycin.
9. Thank you for (you changed) that cheque.
10. After (it moved) out of London, the firm had to pay less rent.

Reading Look at the letter on page 122.

**Language
Points** Note these expressions.

Owing to
We are having difficulty in obtaining
In a position to
Kindly . . .
to call on

THE AUTOMOBILE COMPANY OF AMERICA LTD
274 London Road
LUTON
BEDFORDSHIRE

Telephone: 64789 (STD Code 0531)   Telegrams: AUTUSCO, LUTON

Your ref:
Our ref: ENG/BB/675/22314   17th January, 1972

The Export Sales Manager,
Deutschpneu A.G.,
Friedrichstrasse 479,
Dusseldorf, GERMANY

Dear Sir,

        Supply of Motor Tyres

    Owing to a strike at the factory of our British suppliers, we are
having difficulty in obtaining motor-tyres of the following specification

        520 x 13 4 ply radial.

    We understand you are probably in a position to supply us.   Kindly
instruct your salesman to call on us.

                Yours faithfully,

                K. L. Benson

                K.L. Benson
                Purchasing Manager

Exercise B   You are Mr. K. L. Benson, the Purchasing Manager of the
Automobile Company of America Ltd., in Luton, England.
You want a carpet for the Managing Director's office, but
owing to *an interruption in the supply of* wool, you are unable
to obtain a carpet 6 metres by 5 metres from your normal
supplier. Write to the Sales Manager of Welsh Wool Carpets
Ltd., Address: 569 Newport Road, Cardiff, Glam. and ask
him to instruct a salesman to call on you. Make the necessary
changes to the model letter.

Reading   Look at these letters.

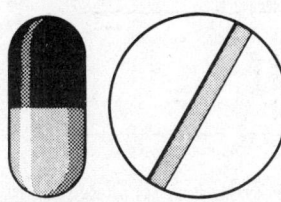

WASHFORD PHARMACEUTICALS LTD
49 Chelmsford Street LONDON W1Y 6BZ

Plaza Hotel,   Telephone: 01-499 7467
Marchant Street,   Telegrams: WASHFORD, LONDON
LIVERPOOL L2   7UD   W.1

Your ref: 14th October, 1972
Our ref: HR/WJ/72/432

Dear Sirs,

    Would you kindly reserve a single room with bath for the nights of
27th and 28th October in the name of Howard Johnson.

    Kindly confirm this reservation.

                Yours faithfully,

                J.E. Green

              J.E. Green (Miss)
              Secretary to the Sales Manager

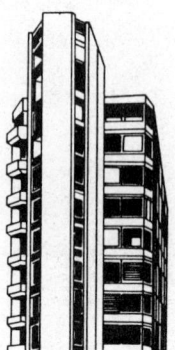

PLAZA HOTEL
Marchant Street LIVERPOOL L2 7UD

Our ref: RES/OCT/27
Your ref: HR/WJ/72/432

Telephone: 051-272 4302
Telegrams: PLAZAHOTEL,
LIVERPOOL

Miss J.E. Green,
Secretary to the Sales Manager,
Washford Pharmaceuticals Ltd.,
49 Chelmsford Street,
LONDON W1Y 6BZ

16th October, 1972

Dear Madam,

    Thank you for your letter of 14th October. We have pleasure in confirming that we are reserving a single room with bath for Mr Howard Johnson for the nights of 27th and 28th October.

                    Yours faithfully,

                    CMBurton

                    C.M. Burton (Mrs)
                    Receptionist for Manager

Exercise C   You are secretary to the Sales Manager of the Automobile Company of America. Write a letter to the Savoy Hotel, Strand, London, W.C.1 asking for the reservation of a double room with bathroom for your boss and his wife for the nights of 24th and 25th May. Your boss's name is Mr Currie.

                    Now you are the receptionist at the Savoy Hotel in London. Write a reply confirming the reservation.

Test for Lessons Thirty-one to Forty

Exercise A   Put *on*, *in*, *at* in the following sentences:

1. We checked in at the hotel .... the night of 24th April.
2. The ship left .... Thursday afternoon.
3. I never go to the cinema .... the afternoon.
4. You cannot park here .... night.
5. The sea is often very rough .... the evening.
6. We are looking forward to your visit .... Wednesday morning.

Exercise B   Today I must leave the office at ten o'clock. First I must go to the post-office, then I must catch a bus. I must arrive at the factory on time.

Now write this passage again beginning with 'Yesterday', not 'Today'.

Exercise C   Look at these sentences.

Type O.   It didn't snow much yesterday.
Type P.   It did. It snowed a great deal.

Type O.   You don't make many telephone calls.
Type P.   I do. I make a great many.

Now turn these Type O sentences into Type P sentences.

1. There weren't many doctors at the conference.
2. The manager can't reduce your salary much.
3. You don't use much toothpaste.
4. We don't receive many free samples.
5. The newsagent hasn't got many customers.

Exercise D   Look at these sentences.

Type O.   The Purchasing Manager's flying to Paris tonight.   (I   her)
Type R.   I told her the Purchasing Manager was flying to Paris tonight.
Type S.   I said the Purchasing Manager was flying to Paris tonight.

Now turn these Type O sentences into Type R and Type S sentences.

1. We can't renew the lease next year.   (The Manager   me)
2. My eldest brother has got a factory.   (I   the secretary)
3. You're famous.   (Your mother   me)
4. Mr Dean is clearing Customs now.   (That man   me)
5. Cosmetics are very expensive in France.   (My friend   her)
6. We're having a discussion about the new products.   (You   my secretary)
7. We're writing you a letter.   (The clerk   you)
8. They always send a circular.   (They   the company)
9. David likes the grey car.   (My sister   me)
10. Her cooking is better than mine.   (My husband   her)

Exercise E Put the correct form of the adjective and supply *than* where necessary.

1. John is (tall) David.
2. That photograph is (good) mine.
3. Donald is the (old) child in the Davis family.
4. Mr Dean's car is (big) of the ones at the factory.
5. You typing is (correct) mine.

Exercise F Look at these sentences.

Type T. First she paid the butcher, then she drove away. (When)
Type U. When she had paid the butcher she drove away.

Now turn these Type T sentences into Type U sentences.

1. First the plane landed, then he went into the Customs. (As soon as)
2. First I cashed the cheque, then I went to the manager's office. (After)
3. First Mr Dean checked in, then he had a shower. (When)
4. First we reduced our costs, then we bought the factory. (before)
5. First the lease came to an end, then we moved to the country. (As soon as)

Exercise G Put the adverb in mid-position in these sentences.

1. He didn't go to the cinema. (often)
2. There is fog in November. (sometimes)
3. This antibiotic ends the illness. (usually)
4. We shall renew the lease. (perhaps)
5. He remembers me. (never)

Exercise H Make the sentences in Exercise G into questions, putting the mid-position adverbs in the correct position.

Exercise I Put the correct form of the verb in these sentences.

1. Thank you for (you entertained) me at that restaurant.
2. I don't object to (I shall renew) the lease.
3. I never go to London without (I visit) the theatre
4. We have pleasure in (we are launching) our new product.
5. What did you do on (you checked in) at the hotel?

Exercise J Read this passage.

Jean is going to drive to the airport; Mr Dean is arriving from Tokyo. If the plane is early, he'll clear Customs before she arrives at the airport. Normally, if Jean telephoned the airline, they'd tell her the plane's time of arrival. But owing to a strike there's nobody at the airline counter, and they don't answer. If Jean goes to the airport without knowing the plane's time of arrival, she'll probably have to wait for a long time. If she has any difficulty in finding a parking-place she will possibly arrive late. But if she doesn't meet Mr Dean, nobody else will be there, because Mrs Dean is in hospital.

Now answer these questions.

1. What will happen if the plane is early?
2. What would happen normally if Jean telephoned the airline?
3. What will probably happen if she goes to the airport without knowing the plane's time of arrival?
4. What will happen if she has any difficulty in finding a parking place?
5. What will happen if Jean doesn't meet Mr Dean?
6. Why isn't Mrs Dean meeting her husband?

Exercise K   Look at these sentences.

Type V.   We aren't moving to the country. We shan't pay less rent.
Type W.   If we moved to the country, we'd pay less rent.

Type V.   He likes me. He brings me flowers.
Type W.   If he didn't like me he wouldn't bring me flowers.

Now turn these Type V sentences into Type W sentences.

1. The newsagent's got a lot of customers. He sells a lot of magazines.
2. There's a strike. They have difficulty in supplying the goods.
3. The boss is not away on a business trip. I can't meet you at the bus-station.
4. I like the Ritz. I always stay there.

Vocabulary introduced in Lessons 31 to 40

(be) able	bed	cash (v)	cooking
absence	best	catch	cosmetics
accident	best wishes	(in) charge	costs
after (conj.)	better	change (v)	country (not town)
agent	big	check (v)	(of) course
always	black	check in	cup
America	body	chief	Customs
announce	boss	circular	decision
apply	business-trip	clear (Customs)	departure
arrangement	bus-station	clothes	different
arrival	by	colour	difficulty
assistant	call on	confirm	discussion
as soon as	capital letter	continue	doctor
automobile	carpet	contract (n)	double

127

during	invite	party	special
elder	item	pass (v)	specification
eldest	kind	perhaps	spend
enclose	kiss (v)	plan (v)	staff
ever	land (v)	(in a) position to	S.T.D.
exactly	large	possible	still (adv)
expensive	learn	post (v)	Stockholm
expression	lease	practice	straight
fabulous	less	(at) present	strike (n)
factory	list (n)	probably	supplier
famous	long	Purchasing	supply (v)
find	longhand	Manager	sure
flat (n)	(a) long time	railway-station	surprising
flight-number	look at (have a)	ready	take out
fog	look forward to	receive	talk (have a)
free	lounge	red	telephone-call
frequently	market (v)	reduce	that's fine
frost	member	ref.	that's a pity
garage	metre	remember	theatre
get out of	model	remove	throw
grateful	motor	renew	till (conj.)
(a) great deal	move	rent	time
(a) great many	necessary	reply (n)	(in) time
green	never	rich	(on) time
grey	next time	road	tired
handle (v)	new	rough	tyre
hard	normal	route	underline
heavy	notice (v)	salary	usually
(at) home	object (v)	sales-manager	visit (n)
hospital	often	sample	wastepaper-basket
idea	old	school	white
if	opinion	sea	wool
ill	order (n)	ship	worse
illness	owing to	shut (v)	worst
instruct	park (v)	single	Yours faithfully
interruption	parking-place	sometimes	Yours sincerely

Conversation Mr Dean and Mr Grant are returning to London by car after visiting several factories in the country.

Mr Dean: Which one did you like best, Jack?

Mr Grant: I liked the factory *which* we saw first, Mr Dean.

Mr Dean: The one *which* stood by the railway?

Mr Grant: Yes. The man *who* is selling it said he wanted to sign a contract quickly. That's the one *which* we shall buy for the lowest price.

Mr Dean: That's quite likely. Who are the estate-agents? The people *whom* we visited in Langford?

Mr Grant: That's right. They were the estate-agents *whom* I liked best, too.

Language Points Look at these sentences.

Mr Grant liked the factory.
They saw it first.
Mr Grant liked the factory which they saw first.

Mr Grant liked the factory.
It stood by the railway.
Mr Grant liked the factory which stood by the railway.

The man was selling it.
He said he wanted to sign a contract quickly.
The man who was selling it said he wanted to sign a contract quickly.

That's the one.
They will buy it for the lowest price.
That's the one which they will buy for the lowest price.

The estate-agents are people.
They visited them in Langford.
The estate-agents are the people whom they visited in Langford.

They were the estate-agents.
Mr Grant liked them best, too.
They were the estate-agents whom Mr Grant liked best, too.

Notice that we use *which* for things, *who* or *whom* for people.
We use *who* as the subject and *whom* for the object of the verb.

Exercise A   Look at these sentences.

Type B.   I read that book.
You bought *it*.

Type C.   I read that book which you bought.

Type B.   The girl was good-looking.
We saw *her* in the cinema.

Type C.   The girl whom we saw in the cinema was good-looking.

Type B.   That man is Swedish.
He says he lives in Brazil.

Type C.   That man who says he lives in Brazil is Swedish.

Now turn the following Type B sentences into Type C sentences.

1. Miss Brown is the secretary. *She* is in charge of the correspondence.
2. You threw the letter into the wastepaper-basket. I had dictated *it*.
3. That typewriter is the best one. *It*'s on the small table.
4. The man is the manager of the company. *He* signed the contract.
5. That girl works for a cosmetics company. You saw *her* here yesterday.
6. The plane arrived late. We went to meet *it*.
7. The firms pay higher salaries. *They* have got their offices in London.
8. The circular advertises a beauty-product. You received *it* yesterday.
9. The man was at the bank yesterday. *He* has no money in his account.
10. The arrangements are better. You made *them* yesterday.
11. Is he staying at the hotel? We liked *it*.
12. That man is here again. You told *him* to go away.
13. The beer wasn't good. We drank *it* in Paris.
14. The car was a Jaguar. Mr Dean wanted to buy *it*.
15. The room is at a new hotel. We had reserved *it* for you.
16. The firm placed an order. *They* wrote to us last week.
17. The member of staff is my secretary. You met *her* here.
18. The man is Mr Grant. *He* will be in charge.
19. The flight leaves at six o'clock. I shall book *it*.
20. The telephone-call was expensive. I made *it*.

Now compare these pairs of sentences. The first in each case appeared after the reading-passage at the beginning of the lesson.

| *Type C.* | Mr Grant liked the factory which they saw first. |
| *Type Z.* | Mr Grant liked the factory that they saw first. |

| *Type C.* | Mr Grant liked the factory which stood by the railway. |
| *Type Z.* | Mr Grant liked the factory that stood by the railway. |

| *Type C.* | The man who was selling it wanted to sign a contract quickly. |
| *Type Z.* | The man that was selling it wanted to sign a contract quickly. |

| *Type C.* | That's the one which they will buy for the lowest price. |
| *Type Z.* | That's the one that they will buy for the lowest price. |

| *Type C.* | The agents were the people whom they visited in Langford. |
| *Type Z.* | The agents were the people that they visited in Langford. |

| *Type C.* | They were the agents whom Mr Grant liked best, too. |
| *Type Z.* | They were the agents that Mr Grant liked best, too. |

 Now do Exercise A again, turning the Type B sentences into Type Z sentences. You can also do this with the examples at the beginning of the exercise.

Exercise B   Listen to your teacher.

Conversation　One Sunday Mr Dean telephoned Jean Brown's house. Her mother answered it. Jean was having a bath. Her mother went to the bathroom-door.

Mother:　Jean, it's Mr Dean. He wants to know whether you can come to the 'phone.

Jean:　Mother, I can't. Ask him if it's urgent.

Mother:　Mr Dean, Jean's asking whether it's urgent.

Mr Dean:　Yes, it is. I've got to fly to Madrid this evening and I can't get Mr Grant on the 'phone. Are you quite sure she can't come to the 'phone?

Mother:　Yes, I am. She's having a bath.

Mr Dean:　Oh, I see. Well would you ask her if she would mind telling Mr Grant tomorrow that I'm in Madrid.

Mother:　Certainly. Jean, he's asking if you'd mind telling Mr Grant that he had to fly to Madrid.

Jean:　No, of course not. Mother, ask him whether there's anything else.

Mother:　Mr Dean, she'd like to know whether there's anything else.

Mr Dean:　Would you ask her whether she typed a letter to Mr Bloom before leaving the office on Friday?

Mother:　Jean, he'd like to know if you typed a letter to Mr Bloom on Friday afternoon.

Jean:　No, I didn't. Ask him when he dictated it.

Mother:　Mr Dean, she says she didn't type the letter. She wants to know when you dictated it.

Mr Dean:　Please tell her I dictated it on Friday morning.

132

Mother: Would you like me to ask her if she knows where it is?

Mr Dean: No, that's all right. She certainly knows where it is. Please forgive me for telephoning while she's having a bath.

Mother: Yes, of course, Mr Dean. I'm sure she doesn't mind. Have a good journey. Goodbye.

Mr Dean: Goodbye Mrs Brown, and thank you.

Language Points

Look at these sentences from the passage.

1.	He wants to know	whether	you can come to the 'phone.
2.	Ask him	if	it's urgent.
3.	Jean's asking	whether	it's urgent.
4.	Well, would you mind asking her	if	she would mind telling Mr Grant tomorrow that I'm in Madrid.
5.	Jean, he's asking	if	You'd mind telling Mr Grant tomorrow that he's in Madrid.
6.	Mother, ask him	whether	there's anything else.
7.	Mr Dean she'd like to know	whether	there's anything else.
8.	Would you ask her	whether	she typed a letter to Mr Bloom?
9.	Jean, he'd like to know	if	you typed a letter to Mr Bloom?
10.	Ask him	when	he dictated it.
11.	She wants to know	when	you dictated it.
12.	Would you like me to ask her	if she knows	where it is?
13.	She certainly knows		where it is.

Now compare the sentences above with the following sentences.

1. Can you come to the 'phone?

2/3. Is it urgent?

4/5. Would ${}^{\text{she}}_{\text{you}}$ mind telling Mr Grant tomorrow that he's in Madrid?

6/7. Is there anything else?

8/9. Did ${}^{\text{she}}_{\text{you}}$ type a letter to Mr Bloom?

10/11. When did ${}^{\text{he}}_{\text{you}}$ dictate it?

12/13. Does she know?
Where is it?

The first list of sentences are indirect questions. The second list consists of direct questions. Notice the difference in word-order and form. Notice also that if the direct question begins with 'where' 'when' or another word of the same type, it also begins the indirect question. If the direct question begins with can/is/would/does/did etc., we must put in 'if' or 'whether'.

Exercise A   Look at these examples.

Type H.   What's she doing?   (Ask him)
Type I.   Ask him what she's doing.

Type H.   Are they arriving on the eight o'clock train?
          (My secretary wants to know)
Type I.   My secretary wants to know if they're arriving on the eight o'clock train.
          Now turn these Type H sentences into Type I sentences, and give the *if* and *whether* forms where possible.

1. Is the General Manager in the factory?   (The boss is asking me)
2. Would you like to have soup first?   (The waiter wants to know)
3. Who do we buy raw materials from?   (The customer is asking us)
4. Where did you buy that coffee?   (My wife wants to know)
5. Can they take an urgent order?   (Would you mind asking them)
6. When did I dictate that letter?   (I want to know)
7. Why couldn't you get him on the 'phone?   (Mr Dean insists on knowing)
8. When will she come out of the bathroom?   (Her husband is tired of asking)
9. Did you buy that in Paris?   (My wife would like to know)
10. Did you have a good journey?   (He wants to know)
11. Do you always stay at the Manhattan Towers Hotel?   (Would you mind telling me)
12. Who looks after the machinery in the factory? (My secretary often asks me)
13. Is the firm moving to the country?   (Mr Grant still doesn't know)
14. Have we got a single room with bathroom on the first floor? (They're asking us)
15. Did they send you a free sample?   (Uncle Jim wants to know)
16. Shall we be able to sell Marvomycin?   (The Advertising Manager doesn't know)

Exercise B   Listen to your teacher.

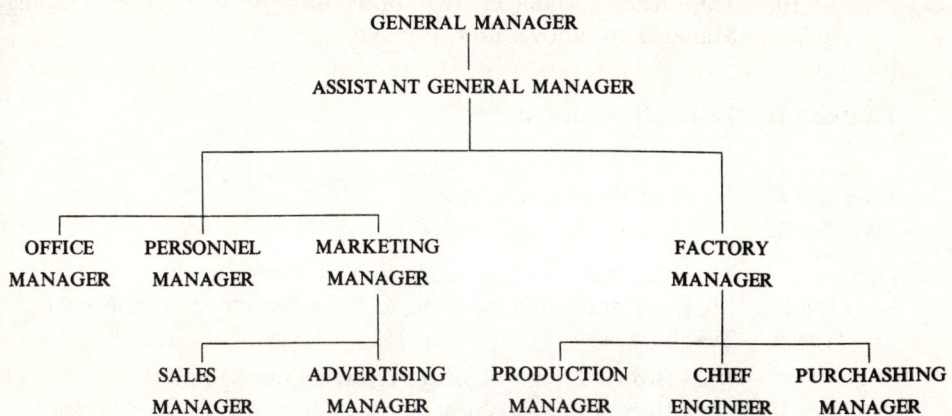

This chart shows the organisation of the executives of a company. It is an organisation-chart.

Exercise A   These are statements about the chart.

Type B.   The General Manager, the Assistant General Manager, the Office Manager and the Factory Manager are senior executives.
Type C.   They're all senior executives.
Type D.   All of them are senior executives.

Type B.   The Sales Manager and the Advertising Manager are responsible to the Marketing Manager.
Type C.   They're both responsible to him.
Type D.   Both of them are responsible to him.

Now express the Type B statements in the form of Type C and Type D statements.

1. The office and the factory are large buildings.
2. The Production Manager, the Chief Engineer and the Purchasing Manager are responsible to the Factory Manager.
3. The executives are responsible to the General Manager.
4. The General Manager and the Assistant General Manager have got their offices on the fifth floor.
5. The Office Manager, the Personnel Manager and the Marketing Manager work in the office building.
6. The Assistant General Manager and the Sales Manager travel a great deal.
7. The Production Manager and the Chief Engineer work in the factory.
8. The Purchasing Manager, the Office Manager and the Personnel Manager have got offices on the third floor.
9. The Assistant General Manager and the Chief Engineer are under thirty years old.

10. The General Manager, the Office Manager and the Purchasing Manager are all over fifty years old.

Exercise B   Listen to your teacher.

Exercise C   Look at these examples.
(Revision)

Mr Dean must take the plane to New York tonight.
Type D.   Mr Dean must take the plane to New York tonight, mustn't he?
Type E.   Yes, he must.

Miss Brown doesn't object to receiving free samples.
Type D.   Miss Brown doesn't object to receiving free samples, does she?
Type E.   No, she doesn't.

Now change the following sentences into Type D and E sentences.

1. Mrs Dean didn't go to Brussels.
2. Your secretary will reserve a room at the Ritz for me.
3. There's an interruption in the supply of Brazilian coffee.
4. Mr Bloom can't meet you at Kennedy Airport.
5. He threw that letter into the wastepaper-basket.
6. This product doesn't remove ugly hair.
7. We launched Penilongin without sending free samples.
8. He'll check in at the Savoy.
9. It hadn't rained when you arrived.
10. Mr Dean didn't have to sell his car.

Conversation   This passage continues the conversation we read between Mr Dean and Mr Grant in Lesson Forty-one.

Mr Grant: Which factory did you like best, Mr Dean?

Mr Dean: I preferred the one we saw last.

Mr Grant: You mean the one we left a few minutes ago?

Mr Dean: That's the one I'm thinking about.

Mr Grant: What was the point you particularly liked about that factory? It's a long way from the railway.

Mr Dean: Yes, but the motorway we came by from London passes near it. After all, the goods we produce are not heavy. But that's a matter we must discuss with the Transport Manager.

Mr Grant: Yes, there are other people we must discuss it with, too.

Language Points   Look at these sentences.

This passage continues the conversation between Mr Dean and Mr Grant. We read the conversation.

This passage continues the conversation *that* we read between Mr Dean and Mr Grant.

This passage continues the conversation we read between Mr Dean and Mr Grant.

Mr Dean preferred the factory.
They saw it last.
Mr Dean preferred the factory *that* they saw last.
Mr Dean preferred the factory they saw last.

Mr Dean means one factory.
They left if a few minutes ago.
Mr Dean means the factory *that* they left a few minutes ago.
He means the one they left a few minutes ago.

Mr Dean is talking about one factory.
That is the one.
That is the one *about which* he is talking.
That's the one *that* he's talking about.
That's the one he's talking about.

Mr Dean particularly liked one point about the factory.
What was the point?
What was the point *that* Mr Dean particularly liked about it?
What was the point he particularly liked about it?

They came from London by a motorway.
The motorway passes near it.
The motorway *by which* they came from London passes near it.
The motorway *that* they came by from London passes near it.
The motorway they came by from London passes near it.

They produce goods.
The goods are not heavy.
The goods *that* they produce are not heavy.
The goods they produce are not heavy.

That's a matter.
They must discuss it with the Transport Manager.
That's a matter *that* they must discuss with the Transport Manager.
That's a matter they must discuss with the Transport Manager.

There are other people.
They must discuss it with them, too.
There are other people *with whom* they must discuss it, too.
There are other people *that* they must discuss it *with*, too.
There are other people they must discuss it with, too.

Notice that we can omit the relative pronoun when it is the object of the verb in the relative clause, or when there is a preposition before the relative pronoun. When the relative pronoun is omitted, the preposition appears after the verb in the relative clause.

Exercise A   Look at these examples.

Type B.   The *motor-tyres* have arrived.
          You supplied *them* to us.
Type C.   The motor-tyres you supplied to us have arrived.

Type B.   That is the *secretary*. I was telling you about *her*.
Type C.   That is the secretary I was telling you about.

Now turn the following Type B sentences into Type C sentences.

138

1. The *factory* will reduce our costs. We are moving to *it*.
2. That short, ugly *man* is our Managing Director. You saw *him* at the hotel last week.
3. The *decision* increased our sales. We made *the decision* last May.
4. The *arrangements* are not possible. You were thinking about *them*.
5. The *factory* produces carpets. My husband is in charge of *it*.
6. No one answered the *letter*. I wrote *it* last week.
7. The *antibiotic* is selling well. We launched *it* last September.
8. The *train* was late. He arrived by *it*.
9. That *hotel* is the best in town. He checked in at *it*.
10. The *goods* will arrive next week. You ordered *them*.
11. Both of the *directors* will travel on the same plane. You reserved a room for *them*.
12. This is a *matter*. We must discuss *it* with the senior executives.
13. The *raw materials* are better. We bought *them* from our Argentinian suppliers.
14. The *man* came in at half-past ten. You telephoned *him*.
15. The *hotel* is very good. We stayed at *the hotel* in New York.
16. The *chart* is here. The Sales Manager will insist on seeing *it*.
17. The *typewriter* is on the large table. You wrote the letter with *it*.
18. These free *samples* are very small. You sent us *them*.
19. The *plane* was late. Mr Dean took *it* from   Paris.
20. The *salaries* are very small. Washford pay *them*.

WICKHAM ENGINEERING CO. LTD

27 Wheat Street 3rd Floor
LONDON EC3H 5XB

Ref: VL/276   23rd January, 1974

Sales Department,
Universal Plastics Ltd.,
74 Norwich Row,
London W9D 5BH

Dear Sirs,

　　Would you kindly despatch to this office as soon as possible the
following goods as per the specification in your catalogue:

　　1 doz. sheets laminate No. 2523 60cm. by 40cm.

　　Please advise the price of these goods, with discount, when we
shall arrange the appropriate remittance.

　　　　　　Yours faithfully,

　　　　　　Vera Lake

　　　　　　Vera Lake (Miss)
　　　　　　Secretary to the Purchasing Manager

Read these two business letters.

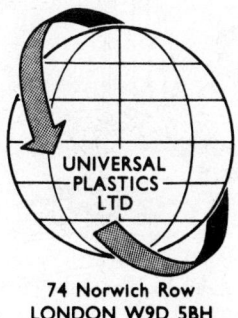

UNIVERSAL PLASTICS LTD

74 Norwich Row
LONDON W9D 5BH

```
Your ref: VL/276                              25th January, 1974
Our ref: 2523/73/912

Miss Vera Lake,
Secretary to the Purchasing
             Manager,
Wickham Engineering Co. Ltd.,
27 Wheat Street,
Third Floor,
London  EC3H 5XB


Dear Madam,

     We are in receipt of your esteemed order of 23rd January, 1974.  We
are dispatching the goods by lorry today and trust that you will receive
them in good order.   Our invoice No. 25846/123 in the amount of £32.50
is attached, and we should be grateful for remittance of the correspond-
ing sum in due course.

                         Yours faithfully,



                         R.J. Jenkins (Mrs)
                         for Sales Manager
```

Exercise B Look at these two letters carefully again and notice the new words and expressions.

Now you are Secretary to the Purchasing Manager of

Southern Studios Ltd
48 High Street
Langford
Herts LG3 7UH

Write to the Sales Manager at

Sunshine Photographic Co.,
272 London Road
Causewell
Middlesex MX3 UW8

and order 2 dozen Fotocolor films, specification 35/36.

Write the reply. The price of the goods is £40.00.

Conversation Here is a conversation between the owner of a small firm and his bank manager.

Manager: Ah, come in, Mr Harris. I'm sorry you had to wait.

Mr Harris: Not at all.

Manager: Do sit down. How are you?

Mr Harris: Fine thank you. How are you?

Manager: Very well thank you. Now what can I do for you?

Mr Harris: Well, we want you to make us a small loan. You see, we had to increase our employees' wages last month, and although we're increasing our prices, too, we're not receiving that money yet.

Manager: Yes, I see. How much do you want us to lend you?

Mr Harris: Five thousand pounds.

Manager: Mm. What security can you offer?

Mr Harris: We have a fixed-period investment in African Aluminium Ltd. We invested £5,000 for one year at seven per cent. It matures in April.

Manager: That's all right. What period do you want us to make the loan for?

Mr Harris: Well, if possible, we want you to allow us to go into overdraft. That will be cheap for us and simple for you.

Manager: Yes, that's fine. As you're an old customer we shan't want you to sign a written contract.

Mr Harris: Well, that's very good of you.

Manager: Not at all, Mr Harris. It was pleasant to see you.

Mr Harris: Well, thank you very much. Good morning.

Manager: Good morning.

<table>
<tr><td>**Language Points**</td><td colspan="3">Study the following sentences from the conversation.</td></tr>
</table>

We want	you	to make us a small loan.
How much do you want	us	to lend you?
What period do you want	us	to make the loan for?
We want	you	to allow us to go into overdraft.
We shan't want	you	to sign a contract.

Exercise A Look at these sentences.

Type Y. Mr Harris said to the bank manager: 'Please give me a loan.'
What did Mr Harris want the bank manager to do?

Type Z. Mr Harris wanted the bank manager to give him a loan.

Now make Type Z sentences from the following Type Y sentences.

1. Mr Harris will say to the bank manager: 'Please allow me to offer my investment as security.'
What will Mr Harris want the bank manager to do?

2. The workers said to the manager: 'Increase our wages.'
What did the workers want the manager to do?

3. Our customer said to us, 'Please send the goods at once.'
What did our customer want us to do?

4. The bank manager says to Mr Dean: 'Would you kindly sign a contract.'
What does the bank manager want Mr Dean to do?

5. My friend will probably say to me: 'Would you lend me some money?'
What will my friend probably want me to do?

6. Her husband said to her: 'Invest that money in Washford Pharmaceuticals at ten per cent.'
What did her husband want her to do?

7. My secretary usually says to me: 'Buy me an expensive bottle of wine.'
What does my secretary usually want me to do?

8. My boss said to me: 'Would you please be responsible for all the correspondence.'
What did my boss want me to do?

9. Mr Grant said to the General Manager: 'Buy the factory near the railway.'
What did Mr Grant want the General Manager to do?

10. Mrs Dean said to Mrs Gray: 'Come to my house for dinner.'
What did Mrs Dean want Mrs Gray to do?

143

11. The children said to Mr Davis: 'Please take us on holiday to Spain.'
What did the children want Mr Davis to do?

12. My boss always says to me: 'Please go to the cinema with me.'
What does my boss always want me to do?

Exercise B   Look at these sentences.

Type N.   Mrs Dean said to her husband: 'Don't go to Paris with Mrs Gray.'
What didn't Mrs Dean want her husband to do?

Type O.   She didn't want him to go to Paris with Mrs Gray.

Now change these Type N sentences into Type O sentences.

1. The boss said to me: 'Don't type that letter yet.'
What didn't the boss want me to do yet?

2. The Assistant General Manager said to the Sales Manager: 'Don't launch that new detergent before next year.'
What didn't the Assistant General Manager want the Sales Manager to do?

3. Jean Brown says to Mr Grant's secretary: 'Don't throw that free sample in the wastepaper-basket.'
What doesn't Jean Brown want Mr Grant's secretary to do?

4. The Factory Manager said to the Sales Manager: 'Don't increase prices before next year.'
What didn't the Factory Manager want the Sales Manager to do?

5. Miss Brown says to John: 'Don't go to the post-office if it rains.'
What doesn't Miss Brown want John to do?

6. Mr Johnson will certainly say to her: 'Don't book at the Ritz Hotel.'
What will Mr Johnson certainly not want her to do?

Exercise C   Listen to your teacher.

Conversation Mr and Mrs Dean are thinking of buying a car. They are at a show-room looking at second-hand cars.

Mrs Dean: I like that little one over there. It's big enough for doing the shopping, but perhaps it isn't fast enough for the motor-way.

Mr Dean: I think it's probably too fast for you to drive. In any case it uses too much petrol, although it's small.

Mrs Dean: What about that big grey one in the corner? Is that one very expensive?

Mr Dean: It's big enough, but convertibles are too expensive to insure. Besides, it probably wouldn't be warm enough in this cold weather.

Mrs Dean: Oh! but look at the price! £2,000 is too much to pay for a second-hand car.

Mr Dean: It would probably be too powerful for you to drive in town.

Mrs Dean: Why do men always think that cars are too powerful for women? The one we have at present isn't too powerful for me.

Mr Dean: No, I agree. But it's too small to drive a long distance, and now we are going to live in the country, we must have a car fast enough to take us to London quickly. After all, I must go into London twice or three times a week, and I don't want to spend too much time travelling.

Mrs Dean: Let's go to another showroom. I don't like any of the cars they've got here.

Look at these sentences.

Type A.	That car's big. We could do the shopping in it.
Type B.	That car's big enough to do the shopping.
	That car's big enough for doing the shopping.
Type A.	It's fast. It's suitable for the motorway.
Type B.	It's fast enough for the motorway.
Type A.	The car we have at present isn't powerful. I would like a more powerful one.
Type B.	The car we have at present isn't powerful enough for us.
Type A.	We must have a fast car. It must be able to take us into London quickly.
Type B.	We must have a car fast enough to take us into London quickly.

Exercise A

Now express these sentences as Type B sentences using *enough.*

1. There isn't much sugar in this coffee. I can't drink it.
2. The Assistant Manager isn't very old. Can he take charge of the factory?
3. Our Argentine customer hadn't got much money. He couldn't pay for the goods.
4. That office is big. We can put two secretaries in there.
5. You didn't make the reservation early. Now we can't get the rooms we want.
6. We handle a lot of correspondence. We can give this secretary a job.
7. There isn't much toothpaste here. The children won't be able to clean their teeth.
8. I didn't have much money. I couldn't pay the butcher.
9. There are a lot of seats in the plane. All our salesmen can travel to Rome together.
10. We've got a lot of telephones. They can handle all the calls we get.

Language
Points

Now look at these sentences.

Type N.	That car's very fast. You probably won't be able to drive it.
Type O.	That car's probably too fast for you to drive.
Type N.	Convertibles are expensive to insure. We can't pay so much.
Type O.	Convertibles are too expensive to insure.
Type N.	£2,000 is a lot of money. We don't want to pay so much for a second-hand car.
Type O.	£2,000 is too much to pay for a second-hand car.
Type N.	It's powerful. You probably wouldn't like driving it in town.
Type O.	It's probably too powerful for you to drive in town.
Type N.	It's small. We wouldn't want to drive it a long distance.
Type O.	It's too small to drive a long distance.

Exercise B   Now express these sentences as Type O sentences using *too*.

1. Rents in London are very expensive. We shan't want to move there.
2. This office is small. It's unsuitable for the General Manager.
3. It's early. We can't launch a new product.
4. Mr Grant is young. He can't be Managing Director.
5. The plane arrived late. Mr Dean couldn't sign the contract.
6. The Savoy Hotel is expensive. It's unsuitable for a secretary to stay at.
7. There are a lot of letters here. Miss Brown can't type all of them.
8. Mrs Gray is fat. She can't get into that car.
9. It's cold. We don't want to go out.
10. I'm very tired. I don't want to go to the cinema.

Exercise C   Rewrite some of these sentences with *too* and some with *enough*.

1. He's very rich. He's the owner of a Rolls Royce.
2. This tea's very hot. I can't drink it.
3. This factory is very large. It's not suitable for our firm.
4. That product is very cheap. It can't be good.
5. The airport is large. All planes can land there.
6. The rent is low. We can pay it.
7. This wine is new. We can't drink it.
8. Our goods are heavy. They can't travel by road.
9. We didn't arrive early. We didn't see the film.
10. The restaurant was very crowded. We couldn't eat there.
11. His English was good. He was able to understand Mr Johnson.
12. The weather's warm. My father can go out.
13. This contract is very difficult. My boss can't understand it.
14. The sea will be very rough. The ship won't be able to leave.
15. Our antibiotic is going to be very cheap. Everybody will buy it.
16. That car is expensive to insure. Our office-boy can't pay so much.
17. The train was very fast. We arrived in time.
18. That filing-cabinet is large. We can put all the correspondence in it.
19. That man is very good-looking. He can't be the Office Manager.
20. My feet are very big. These shoes are unsuitable for me.

Conversation Mr Grant has ordered a new adding-machine, but it hasn't arrived. He calls Vera to his office to ask her about it.

Mr Grant: Vera, has that adding-machine arrived?

Vera: No, Mr Grant, it hasn't come yet.

Mr Grant: Have you telephoned to find out what has happened to it?

Vera: Yes, I telephoned this morning. They say they've packed it and loaded it on to the lorry, and that the lorry has left, but they haven't delivered it yet.

Mr Grant: Have you rung the warehouse? Perhaps it's arrived there.

Vera: Ah, that's a good idea. Can I ring from this telephone. Have they repaired this telephone yet?

Mr Grant: Yes, the engineers repaired it yesterday.

Vera: Excuse me, Mr Grant. Hallo, is that the warehouse? Can you tell me if you've received an adding-machine? You have? Splendid. No, that's all, thank you. Goodbye. Yes, Mr Grant, it arrived at the warehouse ten minutes ago.

Mr Grant: Vera, go to the warehouse and see if they've unpacked it. You haven't sent the cheque for it yet, have you? We must make sure that the machine is not damaged before paying for it.

Language Points Look at these sentences from the passage.

Vera, *has* that adding-machine *arrived*? No, Mr Grant, it *hasn't come* yet.
Have you *telephoned* to find out what *has happened* to it?
They say *they've packed* it and *loaded* it on to the lorry, and that the lorry *has left*, but they *haven't delivered* it yet.

Have you *rung* the warehouse? Perhaps it's (it *has*) *arrived* there. *Have* they *repaired* it yet?
Can you tell me if *you've received* an adding-machine? You *have*?
Vera, go to the warehouse and see if they*'ve unpacked* it.
You haven't sent the cheque for it yet, *have you*?

The verbs in *italics* are in *the present perfect tense*. We use this tense when we are interested in the present effects of a past action. We also use it with adverbs of unfinished time.

Look at these sentences again.

Mr Grant: Have you telephoned to find out what has happened to it?
Vera: Yes, I *telephoned this morning*.

Here Vera uses the past simple tense, because she says *when* she telephoned, and the morning is finished.

Also

Vera: Have they repaired it yet?
Mr Grant: Yes, the engineers *repaired* it *yesterday*.

Vera asks her question in the present perfect tense because she wants to know if the telephone is working now. Mr Grant answers in the past simple tense, because he speaks of yesterday, which is in the past.

Similarly

Vera: It *arrived* at the warehouse *ten minutes ago*.

Notice that questions and negative sentences in the present perfect tense are often used with *yet*, an adverb of unfinished time.

Exercise A   Answer these questions about the conversation.

1.   What has Mr Grant ordered?
2.   Has it arrived at the office yet?
3.   Has Vera telephoned to find out about it?
4.   When did she telephone?
5.   Have they loaded the machine on to the lorry?
6.   Has the lorry left?
7.   Have they received the adding-machine at the warehouse?
8.   When did it arrive?
9.   What does Mr Grant ask Vera about the cheque?
10.   What does Mr Grant tell Vera to make sure?

Exercise B   Listen to your teacher.

Exercise C Look at these sentences.

Type N. Have you booked that room at the hotel? (yesterday)
  or Have you booked that room at the hotel? (last week)
Type O. Yes, I have. I booked it yesterday *or* I booked it last week.

Type N. Has he left for Copenhagen. (not yet)
Type O. No, he hasn't. He hasn't left yet.

Now give Type O answers to the following Type N questions.

1. Have they visited the factory? (not yet)
2. Have they delivered the bicycles? (at ten o'clock this morning)
3. Have we advertised the new product? (on the radio last night)
4. Have you bought me a tube of toothpaste? (not yet)
5. Has the plane landed yet? (ten minutes early)
6. Has the conference finished? (not yet)
7. Has that fixed-period investment matured yet? (a few days ago)
8. Have I dictated that letter about the loan to you? (not yet)
9. Have you eaten at the new restaurant yet? (last Thursday evening)
10. Have you rung the estate-agent? (yesterday afternoon)

Language Points Notice these two sentences.
He has gone to London.
He has been to London.

The first sentence means that he travelled to London, and is still there.
The second sentence means that he went to London, but has now come back, and is here now.

Exercise D Look at these sentences.

Type A. He travelled to London. He is there now.
Type B. He's gone to London.

Type A. He travelled to Madrid, but now he is back.
Type C. He's been to Madrid.

Now turn these Type A sentences into either Type B or Type C sentences. The Type B and C sentences cannot have adverbs of past time in them.

1. He flew to Oslo. He's still there.
2. He went to Morocco, but now he's back.
3. They travelled to Buenos Aires, but now they've returned.
4. We went to Beirut, but now we're back.
5. They flew to Athens, and they're there now.
6. He's not here. He went to Stockholm yesterday.
7. He travelled to Lima, but now he's here again.
8. They went to the Costa Brava last week. They're there now.
9. He isn't here at present. He travelled to Vienna last week.
10. He went to Milan last week, but now he's come back.

150

Conversation   Mr Dean wants to travel to Manchester by train, but it is probable that the railway-workers will go on strike. Mrs Dean is having breakfast when he comes into the dining-room.

Mr Dean: Has the newspaper come yet, my dear?

Mrs Dean: *No, I don't think it has.*

Mr Dean: You know there's probably going to be a strike on the railways, don't you?

Mrs Dean: Yes, when I watched the news last night on the television, *I thought it was probable.*

Mr Dean: You haven't heard the news on the radio this morning, have you?

Mrs Dean: *No, dear, I'm afraid I haven't.* The next bulletin will be at eight o'clock. Do you think the workers will strike?

Mr Dean: *I hope they won't.* The trade-union are demanding a rise of twenty per cent in their wages.

Mrs Dean: Will the management give it to them?

Mr Dean: *I don't think they will.*

Mrs Dean: So the workers will strike.

Mr Dean: *Yes, I'm afraid they will.*

Mrs Dean: Will you have to go to Manchester by plane?

Mr Dean: *Yes, I expect I shall.* Can you drive me to the airport for the two o'clock plane?

Mrs Dean: *I think I can.* Let me look at my diary. Yes, that's all right.

Mr Dean: *I was hoping it was.*

Look at this dialogue. It is the same as the first one with some changes.

Mr Dean: Has the newspaper come yet, my dear?

Mrs Dean: *No, I don't think so.*

Mr Dean: You know there is probably going to be a strike on the railways, don't you?

Mrs Dean: Yes, when I watched the news last night on the television, *I thought so.*

Mr Dean: You haven't heard the news on the radio this morning, have you?

Mrs Dean: *No, dear, I'm afraid not.* The next bulletin will be at eight o'clock. Do you think the workers will strike?

Mr Dean: *I hope not.* The trade-union are demanding a rise of twenty per cent in their wages.

Mrs Dean: Will the management give it to them?

Mr Dean: *I don't think so.*

Mrs Dean: So the workers will strike.

Mr Dean: *Yes, I'm afraid so.*

Mrs Dean: Will you have to go to Manchester by plane?

Mr Dean: *Yes, I expect so.* Can you drive me to the airport for the two o'clock plane?

Mrs Dean: *I think so.* Let me look at my diary. Yes, that's all right.

Mr Dean: *I was hoping so.*

Language Points	Compare the expressions in italics in the two dialogues above.

Has the newspaper come yet, my dear?

Type A.   *No, I don't think it has.*

Type B.   *No, I don't think so.*

You know there's probably going to be a strike on the railways, don't you?

Type A.   When I watched the news last night on the television, *I thought it was probable.*

Type B.   When I watched the news last night on the television, *I thought so.*

You haven't heard the news on the radio this morning, have you?

Type A.   *No, I'm afraid I haven't.*

Type B.   *No, I'm afraid not.*

Do you think the workers will strike?

Type A.   *I hope they won't.*

Type B.   *I hope not.*

Will the management give it to them?

| Type A. | *I don't think they will.* |
| Type B. | *I don't think so.* |

So the workers will strike.

| Type A. | *Yes, I'm afraid they will.* |
| Type B. | *Yes, I'm afraid so.* |

Will you have to go to Manchester by plane?

| Type A. | *Yes, I expect I shall.* |
| Type B. | *Yes, I expect so.* |

Can you drive me to the airport for the two o'clock plane?

| Type A. | *I think I can.* |
| Type B. | *I think so.* |

Yes, that's all right.

| Type A. | *I was hoping it was.* |
| Type B. | *I was hoping so.* |

Notice that we can repeat the auxiliary, *shall, will, have, was,* etc., in these expressions, or we can use a form with *so* or *not*.

Notice that we don't usually say:

	I think not,
BUT	I don't think so
AND ALSO	

$$I \text{ don't think} \begin{cases} \text{he is} \\ \text{they were} \\ \text{she has} \\ \text{I shall} \\ \text{etc.} \end{cases}$$

We do not say *yes* or *no* if we don't know anything about the subject.

Exercise A   Look at these sentences.

Type Z.	Will the workers go on strike? (afraid yes)
Type A.	Yes, I'm afraid they will
Type Z.	Has the adding-machine arrived? (think no)
Type A.	No, I don't think it has.
Type Z.	Will they reserve us a room at the Ritz? (hope no)
Type A.	I hope they won't.

Now turn the following Type Z sentences into Type A sentences.

1. Is he one of the firm's executives? (think   yes)
2. Has he been to Barcelona? (afraid   no)
3. The workers aren't on strike are they? (hope   no)

4. His wife's Brazilian, isn't she? (think no)
5. Does this car belong to the managing director? (think yes)
6. Will the bus arrive in time? (hope yes)
7. Have you finished that bottle of wine? (afraid yes)
8. They are waiting for us at the airport, aren't they? (expect yes)
9. Shall we get our rise in wages? (afraid no)
10. Is there a news-bulletin before ten o'clock? (think no)
11. Has she gone to bed yet? (hope yes)
12. Do you think she's been to the butcher's? (expect yes)
13. She hasn't had breakfast yet, has she? (think no)
14. Are you looking forward to your holidays? (afraid no)
15. My secretary's on holiday. You'll have to write the letter in long-hand. (afraid yes)
16. There's a good road from Venice to Milan, isn't there? (expect yes)
17. You didn't buy a packet of razor-blades, did you? (afraid no)
18. Do you think the bank-manager will give us that loan? (hope yes)
19. Do you think we shall have any difficulties in the Customs? (hope no)
20. Did they invite your boss to the conference? (think yes)
21. Did he have to go to hospital? (afraid yes)

Exercise B Look at these sentences.

Type Z. Will the workers go on strike? (afraid yes)
Type B. Yes, I'm afraid so.

Type Z. Has the adding-machine arrived? (think no)
Type B. No, I don't think so.

Type Z. Will they reserve us a room at the Ritz? (hope no)
Type B. I hope not.

Now do EXERCISE A again, but turn the Type Z sentences into Type B sentences.

Exercise C Listen to your teacher.
Answer his/her questions with one of these answers.

I think so.
I don't think so.
I'm afraid so.
I'm afraid not.
I hope so.
I hope not.
I expect so.

Conversation   Mr Grant is seeing Mr Dean about a financial matter.

Mr Grant: *May* I come in and talk to you about a personal, financial matter, Mr Dean?

Mr Dean: Yes, of course, Jack, go ahead. I'm not very busy at the moment. I *may* get a telephone-call from Oslo, but I don't think it will come through yet.

Mr Grant: Well, I want to invest some money on the stock-exchange. If I don't consult someone who knows about it, I *might* lose a lot of money.

Mr Dean: *May* I ask how much you have to invest?

Mr Grant: I *may* have about a thousand pounds by the end of the month.

Mr Dean: Well, of course, nothing on the stock-exchange is ever certain. But if I *may* give you a piece of advice, I think you *might* put £500 into a Unit Trust. Put the other £500 into something less secure which *might* make you a lot of money more quickly. You *might* put your money into African Aluminium, for example.

Mr Grant: Ah yes, somebody told me that their shares *may* go up. Their dividend was low this year, wasn't it?

Mr Dean: Yes, that's why the price has come down. But the prospects of the company are very good. They *may* not give a good dividend next year either, but that's not the point. The point is that the value of the shares *may* increase.

Mr Grant: What do you think of Northern Trading Company, Mr Dean? I thought I *might* put a part of my money into that.

Mr Dean: Don't do that. I had lunch with their Sales Manager the other day, and he told me in confidence that he's afraid they *may* go bankrupt.

Notice that we use *may* in two ways in this dialogue. Here are two examples of the first. Here, *may* has the same meaning as *can*.

Mr Grant says: *May* I come in and talk to you?
Mr Dean says: *May* I ask how much you have to invest?
                  If I *may* give you a piece of advice . . .

Notice that Mr Dean answers Mr Grant's question by saying 'Of course, go ahead.' We do not usually say 'Yes, you may.' The two forms we usually meet in this sense are:

> *May I?*
> *May we?*

Other forms are not usual. The usual affirmative answer is:
> Yes, of course.

if only an answer is asked for. (Response 1.)
> Yes, of course, go ahead.

if permission for an action is asked for. (Response 2.)
and
> Of course, thank you very much.

if the request is an invitation. (Response 3.)

Exercise A   Look at these sentences.

Response 1.
Type B. Will you let me go out?
Type C. May I go out?
Type D. Yes, of course, go ahead.

Response 2.
Type B. I want your permission to sign this cheque.
Type C. May I sign this cheque?
Type D. Yes, of course, go ahead.

Response 3.
Type B. Please allow us to invite you to dinner.
Type C. May we invite you to dinner?
Type D. Yes, of course. Thank you very much.

Now turn these Type B sentences into Type C sentences and give the Type D answer.

1. Please allow me to ask you a question in confidence.
2. I want your permission to invite you to lunch.
3. Please let me ask your secretary to take this letter.
4. Please allow us to give you a piece of advice.
5. We want your permission to put the car in the garage.
6. Please allow me to make a telephone-call to Barcelona.

7.   Please let me ask you if you have insured the factory.
8.   I want your permission to travel there by air.
9.   Please allow me to have your telephone number.
10. Please let me ask you what your salary is at present.

(Your teacher will tell you how to say 'No' politely to requests beginning *May I/May we*.)

Exercise B   Listen to your teacher.

Language Points   Now look at the way in which we use *may* and also how we use *might*. Here, they are used to talk about possibilities.

I *may* get a telephone call from Oslo.
I *might* lose a lot of money.
I *may* have about a thousand pounds by the end of the month.
You *might* put £500 into a Unit Trust.
Put the other £500 into something less secure which *might* make you a lot of money more quickly.
You *might* put your money into African Aluminium.
Their shares *may* go up.
They *may not* give a good dividend next year.
I *might* put a part of my money into that.
They *may* go bankrupt.

Notice that the negative forms are:

May not
Might not

We use *may* or *might* to talk about possibilities in the future. We use *may* for possibilities of 50% or above, and *might* for possibilities of less than 50%. We also use *might* for polite suggestions. We almost never use question forms of *may* and *might* to talk about possibilities.

Exercise C   Look at these sentences.

Type S.   It is possible that he will not invest his money in aluminium.
Type T.   He may not invest his money in aluminium.

Type S.   It is possible that I shall receive a telegram from our agent in Tokyo, but
            I don't think so
            I'm not sure
            I'm not certain.
Type T.   I might receive a telegram from our agent in Tokyo.

Type S.   I suggest that you listen to his advice.
Type T.   You might listen to his advice.

157

Now turn these Type S sentences into Type T sentences.

1. It is possible that the boss will buy a new adding-machine, but I don't think so.
2. It is possible that we shall find a parking-place near the bus station.
3. I suggest that you put your money into a Unit Trust.
4. It is possible that we shall sign the contract next month.
5. I suggest that you advertise this product.
6. It is possible that his secretary doesn't know shorthand, but I'm not certain.
7. It is possible that he hasn't got any securities.
8. It is possible that he will have dinner with them, but I'm not sure.
9. I suggest that you make a decision tomorrow.
10. It is possible that you will have difficulties with the Customs.
11. It is possible that they will deliver the adding-machine tomorrow.
12. It is possible that this is a free sample, but I don't think so.
13. I suggest that we increase his salary.
14. It is possible that he will not ask us for a decision.
15. It is possible that that is the point, but I don't think so.
16. It is possible that she won't be late for work.
17. It is possible that the aluminium shares will not come down, but I'm not certain.
18. I suggest that you put your money into something more secure.
19. It is possible that the bank will not give you an overdraft.
20. It is possible that the company will increase the dividend next year, but I don't think so.
21. It is possible that the workers will go on strike.
22. It is possible that the firm will not go bankrupt.
23. I suggest that we invest in a company with better prospects.
24. It is possible that he will tell me about the value of his investments in confidence.
25. It is possible that that is the point.

Reading   Miss Brown is trying to obtain an air-passage to New York for Mr Dean. She is telephoning the airlines.

Miss Brown: Hullo, is that International Airlines? May I speak to Extension Number 24? Ah, hullo, Caroline, is that you? Is that Extension 24? Oh, it's 74. Could you give me the switchboard again, please? Ah, Switchboard, I wanted Extension 24, and you gave me 74. Yes, 24. Thank you. Hullo, is that Caroline? Oh, I'm sorry, may I speak to Caroline?* .... Caroline? Oh, good, at last. Jean Brown speaking. *I've had* a lot of trouble getting through to you. Your operator gave me the wrong extension. Listen, Caroline, *you've got* to help me. *Mr Dean's got* to fly to New York as soon as possible. You said the other day when *we were having* lunch together that you might be able to help if *I was having* trouble. All the other airlines are booked up. *Have you got* a cancellation? *You have?* Splendid. No, the company *hasn't got* an account with you. I'll send the office-boy with a cheque to fetch the ticket. What time did you say the plane takes off? Twenty-two thirty. Yes, that's fine. What time *has he got to* check in at the Airport? Half an hour earlier. Right. *The boss has got* an awful cold at the moment. I hope it won't get worse. .... Listen, Caroline, *we're having* a party at Vera's flat next Tuesday. Can you come? *Have you got* Vera's address? *You have?* Good. All right, ring back when *you've got* time. Thanks for getting that passage for me. Nice to hear you, Caroline. *I've got to* ring off now. Bye-bye for now. Goodbye.

We now give the same passage, from the point * where Jean *gets through to* Caroline. Look at the forms of the verb 'to have'.

Miss Brown: *Caroline? Oh good, at last. Jean Brown speaking. *I've had* a lot of trouble in getting through to you. Your operator gave me the wrong extension. Listen, Caroline, *you have to* help me. *Mr Dean has to* fly to New York as soon as possible. You said the other day when *we were having* lunch together that you might be able to help me if *I was having* trouble. All the other airlines are booked up. *Do you have* a cancellation? *You do?* Splendid. No, the company *doesn't have* an account with you. I'll send the office-boy with a cheque to fetch the ticket. What time did you say the plane takes off? Twenty-two thirty. Yes, that's fine. What time *does he have to* check in at the airport? Half an hour earlier? Right. The boss *has* an awful cold at the moment. I hope it won't get worse. . . . . Listen, Caroline, *we're having* a party at Vera's flat next Tuesday. Can you come? *Do you have* Vera's address? *You do?* Good. All right, ring back when *you have* time. Thanks for getting that passage for me. Nice to hear you, Caroline. I *have to* ring off now. Bye-bye for now. Goodbye.

Language points

Compare these two versions of Jean Brown's conversation with Caroline.

In the first she says:

*You've got to help me	*You have to help me.
*Mr Dean's got to fly to New York	*Mr Dean has to fly to New York.
Have you got a cancellation? You have?	Do you have a cancellation? You do?
The company hasn't got an account with you.	The company doesn't have an account with you.
*What time has he got to check in at the airport?	*What time does he have to check in at the airport?
The boss has got an awful cold.	The boss has an awful cold.
Have you got Vera's address? You have?	Do you have Vera's address? You do?
Ring back when you've got time.	Ring back when you have time.
*I've got to ring off now.	*I have to ring off now.

Notice that in the cases marked with an asterisk *, she could also say:

You *must* help me.
Mr Dean *must* fly to New York.
What time *must* he check in at the airport?
I *must* ring off now.

Exercise A   Look at these sentences.

Type B.   He must fly to Tokyo today.
Type C.   I beg your pardon.
Type D.   I said he's got to fly to Tokyo today.
Type E.   Has he really got to?
Type F.   Yes, he really must.

Type B.   I must get through to Caroline.
Type C.   I beg your pardon.
Type D.   I said I've got to get through to Caroline.
Type E.   Have you really got to?
Type F.   Yes, I really must.

Now give Type C, D, E and F responses to these Type B sentences.

1.   She must obtain some new headphones for the dictaphone.
2.   I must buy some scissors.
3.   I must meet her at the cinema.
4.   He must buy some petrol before going on to the motorway.
5.   He must ask the bank-manager for a loan.
6.   She must handle all the telephone calls next Wednesday.
7.   I must give the cleaning-woman a rise in wages.
8.   I must buy a bottle of whisky before the Sales Conference.
9.   She must ring the airport and ask if there's any fog.
10.   He must park his car near the bus-station.
11.   I must have a talk with the Marketing Manager before his departure.
12.   She must telephone the estate-agent and ask about that factory.

Now look at the sentences without asterisks.

Exercise B   Look at these sentences.

Type T.   He's got an awful cold.
Type U.   I'm sorry, what did you say?
Type V.   I said he has an awful cold.
Type W.   Has he? That's the first time you've told me.

Now give Type U, V and W responses to these sentences.

1.   We've got a new operator on the switchboard.
2.   I haven't got an extension in my office.

3. He's got a lot of investments in aluminium.
4. She hasn't got a tube of toothpaste.
5. He's got a house in Switzerland.
6. They've got a new product for removing hair.
7. They haven't got a factory-manager at the moment.
8. The house hasn't got a garage.
9. My secretary hasn't got a husband.
10. The hotel's got a lift.
11. The company have got a showroom in the middle of London.
12. She hasn't got her spectacles in her handbag.
13. He's got an old American convertible.
14. We've got a good-looking red-haired receptionist.
15. He hasn't got good securities.
16. I haven't got any writing paper.
17. He's got a red carpet in his office.
18. We've got some new machinery at the factory.
19. All the men have got heavy suitcases.
20. He's got an ugly elder sister.

Language Points Look back at Jean Brown's conversation on pages 159 and 160. Some expressions with *have* were the same in both versions.

I've had a lot of trouble in getting through to you.
The other day when we *were having* lunch together you said you might be able to help if *I was having* trouble.
We're having a party at Vera's flat next Tuesday.

Compare these with the expressions in Lesson 19 on page 54.

Exercise C You can change some of the following sentences to the *have got* form, but not all of them. Where you can change them, do so, like this, adding a question-tag.

Type X. They have an arrangement with a Brazilian company.
Type Y. They've got an arrangement with a Brazilian company, haven't they?

Type X. He hasn't a bottle of wine in the house.
Type Y. He hasn't got a bottle of wine in the house, has he?

Where you cannot change them, say so, but add a question-tag.

Type V. They're having a good time.
Type W. They're having a good time, aren't they?

Type V. He has a glass of beer every evening.
Type W. He has a glass of beer every evening, doesn't he?

1. He was having lunch at that restaurant.
2. He has lunch at that hotel every Wednesday.
3. They have an account with International Airlines.
4. He has a cigarette as soon as he gets out of bed.
5. You have a bunch of bananas in your bag.
6. She has a husband in Brussels and another in Madrid.
7. He has a baby brother who is only a year old.
8. He's having a cup of coffee at the moment.
9. You have time to make a cancellation.
10. They're having bad weather in Spain at present.
11. He has a shop in Paris which sells shoes.
12. We haven't an operator for our switchboard at present.
13. The company have a Sales Conference in a different town every year.
14. They haven't much money.
15. I have an account at that bank.
16. He always has his whisky and soda with ice.
17. He has an uncle who lives in Singapore.
18. You have a rest after lunch every day.
19. They have a new antibiotic on the market.
20. He has a big, powerful car.
21. We have a plane which leaves at 14.30 hours.
22. The boss is having a look at a factory in Beirut.
23. The hotel hasn't a lounge.
24. He usually has an orange for breakfast.
25. We haven't enough petrol to travel by the motorway.

Exercise D   Listen to your teacher.

Vocabulary introduced in Lessons 41 to 50

account
adding-machine
advertising
advice
advise
ago
aluminium
appropriate
attached
awful
bankrupt
besides
booked up
building
bulletin
call
(in any) case
catalogue
certain
chart
cheap
cold (disease)
come down
come in
come through
  (telephone calls)
(in) confidence
consult
convertible (car)
damaged
deliver
demand
despatch
dining-room
discount
distance
dividend
(in) due course
employee
engineer
enough
estate-agents
esteemed
executive

expect
extension
  (telephone)
(in) fact
(yours) faithfully
fast
fetch
financial
fix
fixed-period
forgive
General Manager
go ahead
go back
go out
go up
hallo
help (v)
here you are
hope
house
increase (v)
insist
insure
international
invest
investment
invoice
last
let
load (v)
loan
lorry
low
machine
Madrid
management
marketing
matter (n)
mature (v)
may
might
motorway
news

obtain
offer (v)
operator
organisation
overdraft
owner
pack (v)
particularly
party
period
per cent
permission
personal
personnel
petrol
pleasant
(the) point (is)
(that's not the) point
pound (money)
powerful
price
produce (v)
production
prospect
radio
raw
receipt
remittance
repair (v)
responsible
ring (telephone)
ring back
rise (n)
second-hand
secure
security
senior
share (investment)
showroom
simple
smile (v)
splendid
stock-exchange
strike (v)

suggest
suggestion
suitable
sum
switchboard
take off (aircraft)
television
trade-union
trading
trouble
trust (v)
try
twice
unit-trust
unpack
unsuitable
urgent
value
wages
warehouse
whether
worker

List of Vocabulary Items

A

able (to be)
about
absence
accident
account
across
adding-machine
address
advertise
advertising
advice
advise
afraid (to be)
after
afternoon
afterwards
again
agency
agent
ago
airline(s)
airline-office
air-passage
airport
allow
all right
aluminium
always
a.m.
America
American
Amsterdam
another
announce
answer
antibiotic
anything
April
apply
appropriate
Argentina
Argentine
arrangement

arrival
arrive
ashtray
ask
asleep
assistant
as soon as
at
attached
Athens
at once
August
automobile
away
awful

B

baby
back (of a building, etc.)
bad
bag
banana
bank
bankrupt
bar (for drinks)
bar (of soap)
barman
Barcelona
bath
bathroom
beach
bed
beer
before
begin
beginning
behind
Beirut
Belgian
belong
besides
best
best wishes

better
between
bicycle
big
black
blackboard
blue
body
book (n)
book (v)
booked up
booking-clerk
boss
bottle
box
boy
Brazil
Brazilian
bread
break
bring
British
brother
brown
Brussels
building
bulletin
bunch
bus
bus station
business
business-friend
businessman
business-trip
busy
butcher's
Buenos Aires
buy
by
bye-bye

C

cafe
cake

call
call on
cancel
cancellation
capital letter
car
carefully
carpet
case (in any)
cash (v)
cashier
catalogue
catch
ceiling
certain
certainly
chair
chalk
change (v)
chart
cheap
check (v)
check in
chemist
cheque
chief
child
chips
chocolate
cigarette
cinema
circular
class
clean (v)
cleaning-woman
clear (customs)
clerk
clock
clock (v)
clothes
cloudy
coat
coffee
cold (disease)

cold (temperature)
colour
come
come down
come (from)
come in
come through
   (telephone calls)
company
complete (v)
conference
(in) confidence
confirm
consult
contact (v)
the Continent
continue
contract (n)
conversation
convertible (car)
cooking
Copenhagen
corner
correctly
correspond (v)
correspondence
cosmetics
costs
count (v)
counter
country (not town)
(of) course
cover (v)
crowded
cup
customer
Customs

D
damaged
dark
daughter
day
daytime
(a great) deal (of)
dear

December
decision
deliver
demand
departure
desk
despatch
detergent
dialogue
diary
dictaphone
dictate
different
difficulty
dining-room
dinner
discount
discuss
discussion
distance
dividend
doctor
door
double
dozen
dress (n)
dress (v)
drink (v)
drive (v)
(in) due course
during

E
early
earn
eat
edge
egg
either
elder
eldest
employee
enclose
end
engineer
engineering

England
English
Englishman
Englishwoman
enough
entertain
envelope
estate-agents
esteemed
Europe
ever
evening
every
everybody
every day
every morning
every time
everywhere
exactly
example
(for) example
except
excuse me
executive
exercise
expect
expensive
expression
extension
   (telephone)
eye

F
fabulous
(in) fact
factory
fair
(yours) faithfully
famous
far
fashion
fast
fat
father
February
fetch

few
file
filing-cabinet
film
financial
find
(that's) fine
fine, thank you
finish
firm (n)
first
fix
fixed-period
flat (apartment)
flight
flight-number
floor (storey)
florist
flour
flower
fly (v)
fog
(the) following
foot
for
forget
forgive
form
France
free
French
Frenchman
Frenchwoman
frequently
Friday
friend
front
frost

G
garage
General Manager
gentleman
get
get off
get on

get out of	here	invoice	like (conj)
get through to	here you are	italics	Lima
get up	hers	Italian	list
glass	his	Italy	listen to
girl	holiday	item	little
give	(on) holiday		(a) little
go	(at) home	**J**	load (v)
go ahead	hope (v)	January	loaf
go back	hospital	job	loan
go out	hot	journey	London
go up	hotel	July	long
good	hour	June	longhand
Good afternoon	house	just now	(a) long (time)
Goodbye	How are you?		(a) long way
Good evening	How do you do?	**K**	look
good-looking	How long?	kilo	look after
Good morning	hurry (in a)	kind (adj)	look at
Goodness!	husband	kindly	(have) a look (at)
Goodnight		kiss (v)	look for
goods		know	look forward to
good time (have a)	**I**		lorry
gossip (person)	I beg your pardon	**L**	(a) lot (of)
grateful	ice	lady	lounge
Great Britain	ice-cream	land	low
(a) great deal	idea	land (v)	Lucerne
(a) great many	if	large	lunch (n)
Greece	ill	(at) last	
Greek	illness	last	**M**
green	I'm sorry	late	machine
greengrocer	immediately	launch (v)	machinery
grey	in	learn	Madam
grocer	increase (v)	lease (n)	Madrid
	in front of	leave	make
	ink	left	make sure
H	insist	lend	mail (n)
half past	insure	less	magazine
hallo	instruct	lesson	man
handle (verb)	It doesn't matter	let	manager
handbag	international	let's get down to	managing director
happen	interruption	business	management
hard	into	let me see	Manchester
hat	in the middle	letter	many
headphones	introduce	light	(a great) many
hear	invest	light?	map
Heavens!	investment	lift	March
heavy	invite	like (v)	market (n)
help (v)			

market (v)	New York	(the) other (day)	plane
marketing	next	ours	pleasant
mask	next time	out of town	please
match (n)	nice	over	(with) pleasure
matter (n)	Nice to see you	overdraft	p.m.
mature (v)	(at) night	owing to	(that's not the) point
may	nighttime	owner	(the) point (is)
May	nobody		that's not the point
meat	noon	**P**	policy
meet	normal	pack (v)	polite
metre	not at all	packet	porter
member	notice (v)	pad	Portugal
midday	No, thank you	page	Portuguese
middle	nothing	pair	(in a) position (to)
might	not just now	Paris	possible
Milan	November	park (v)	post (v)
milk	now	parking-place	poster
mind (v)	(for) now	part	post office
mine	number	particularly	potato
minute (n)		party	pound (money)
model	**O**	pass	powerful
moment	object	passage	practice
(at the) moment	obtain	passport	prefer
Monday	o'clock	past	(at) present
money	October	pavement	price
month	offer (v)	pay (v)	probable
morning	office	pea	probably
Morocco	office-boy	pen	produce (v)
motor	often	pencil	product
mother	old	people	production
motorway	on	perhaps	programme
move (v)	once	period	prospect
much	once a week	per cent	purchasing
must	(at) once	permission	purchasing
	on the left	person	manager
N	on the right	personal	put
name	only	personnel	
nationality	open (v)	petrol	**Q**
near	operator	photograph	(a) quarter past
necessary	opinion	picture	(a) quarter to
neighbour	orange	piece	question
never	order (n)	(it's a) pity	question-tag
new	order (v)	pipe (for smoking)	quickly
news	organization	place (n)	Quite well, thanks
newsagent	Oslo	place (v)	
newspaper	other	plan (v)	**R**
			radio

(by) rail
railway
railway station
rain (v)
razor-blade
raw
read
ready
really
receipt
receive
receptionist
red
red-haired
reduce
ref.
remember
remittance
remove
renew
rent (n)
repair (v)
reply
reserve
reservation
responsible
rest (have a)
rest (remainder)
restaurant
return
rice
rich
right
ring (telephone)
ring back
ring off
rise (n)
road
Rio de Janeiro
room
rough
route
rudely

S
safe (n)

salad
salary
sales
salesman
sales manager
sales policy
same
same to you
sample
Santiago
Saturday
say
school
scissors
sea
second-hand
secretary
secure
security
see
sell
send
senior
sense
sentence
September
share (investment)
shave
shelf
shine
ship
shoe
shop
shop-assistant
(do the) shopping
short
shorthand
show
shower (bath)
showroom
shut
sign
simple
sincerely (yours)
single
Sir

Singapore
sister
sit
sit down
sleep (v)
slow
slowly
small
smile (v)
smoke (v)
snow (n)
soap
sometimes
soda
son
soon
(as) soon (as)
(to be) sorry
sort
soup
Spain
Spaniard
Spanish
speak
special
specification
spectacles
spend (money)
spend (time)
splendid
staff
stamp
stand
stand up
start
statement
station
stay
steak
still
stock
stock-exchange
story
Stockholm
straight
street

strike (n)
strike (v)
student
success
sugar
suggest
suggestion
suitcase
suitable
sum
sun
Sunday
supplier
supply (v)
sure
surprising
Swede
Sweden
Swedish
switchboard
(have a) swim
Switzerland

T
table
take
take off (aircraft)
take out
take place
talk (n)
talk (v)
(have a) talk (with)
tall
tea
teacher
telegram
telephone (n)
telephone (v)
telephone-call
television
tell
that's fine
that's a pity
thank you very
    much
theatre

then	train	**V**	wife
there	travel	value	window
theirs	travel-agency	very well	wine
thin	tray	Venice	(please give my
thing	trouble	Vienna	best) wishes to
think	trousers	view	with
thousand	trust	visit (v)	without
throw	try	visitor	with pleasure
thunderstorm	tube		wool
Thursday	Tuesday	**W**	woman
ticket	twice	wages	work (n)
till	type (print, n)	wait for	work (v)
time	type (v)	waiter	worker
(in) time (for)	typewriter	walk	world
(on) time	typist	wall	worse
timetable	tyre	want	worst
tin (container)		warehouse	write
tired		warm	writer
tobacco	**U**	wastepaper-basket	writing-paper
tobacconist's	ugly	way	wrong
today	umbrella	weather	
together	uncle	Wednesday	**Y**
Tokyo	under	week	year
tomato	underline	well	yellow
tomorrow	understand	western	yesterday
tonight	United States	Western Europe	yet
too (as well)	unit trust	What time?	young
too (excessively)	unpack	when	yours
tooth	unsuitable	whether	Yours faithfully
toothpaste	urgent	while	Yours sincerely
town (out of)	urgently	whisky	
trade-union	use (v)	white	**Z**
trading	usually	wholesaler	Zurich

List of Irregular Verbs

Principal parts of root-changing and irregular verbs appearing in Book One.

present simple	past simple	past participle
begin	began	begun
break	broke	broken
bring	brought	brought
buy	bought	bought
can	could	—
catch	caught	caught
come	came	come
do	did	done
drink	drank	drunk
drive	drove	driven
eat	ate	eaten
find	found	found
fly	flew	flown
forget	forgot	forgotten
forgive	forgave	forgiven
get	got	got
give	gave	given
go	went	gone
have	had	had
hear	heard	heard
know	knew	known
learn	learnt	learnt
leave	left	left
lend	lent	lent
let	let	let
make	made	made
may	might	—
meet	met	met
must	had to	had to
pay	paid	paid
put	put	put
read	read	read
ring	rang	rung
say	said	said
see	saw	seen
sell	sold	sold
send	sent	sent
shine	shone	shone
shut	shut	shut
sit	sat	sat
sleep	slept	slept

present simple	past simple	part participle
speak	spoke	spoken
spend	spent	spent
stand	stood	stood
strike	struck	struck
take	took	taken
tell	told	told
think	thought	thought
throw	threw	thrown
understand	understood	understood
write	wrote	written